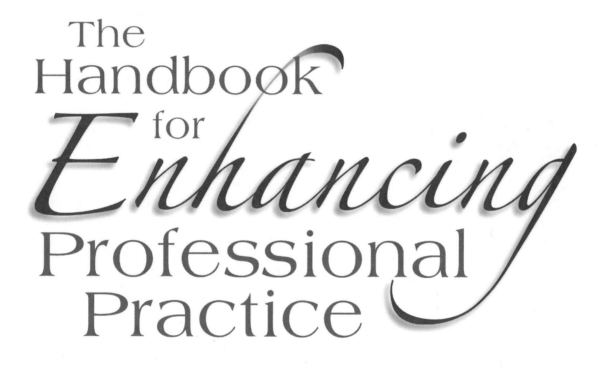

The Handbook for *Enhancing* Professional Practice

Other books by Charlotte Danielson

Enhancing Professional Practice: A Framework for Teaching, 2nd edition (2007) by Charlotte Danielson

Teacher Leadership That Strengthens Professional Practice (2006) by Charlotte Danielson

Enhancing Student Achievement: A Framework for School Improvement (2002) by Charlotte Danielson

An Introduction to Using Portfolios in the Classroom (1997) by Charlotte Danielson and Leslye Abrutyn

Teacher Evaluation to Enhance Professional Practice (2000) by Charlotte Danielson and Thomas L. McGreal

Also available as a download from ASCD, *Electronic Forms and Rubrics for Enhancing Professional Practice: A Framework for Teaching.* Go to ascd.org, select online store, then click on downloads.

The

Handbook
for

Enhancing
Professional
Practice

Using the Framework for Teaching
in Your School

CHARLOTTE DANIELSON

Association for Supervision and Curriculum Development • Alexandria, Virginia USA

Association for Supervision and Curriculum Development
1703 N. Beauregard St. • Alexandria, VA 22311-1714 USA
Phone: 800-933-2723 or 703-578-9600 • Fax: 703-575-5400
Web site: www.ascd.org • E-mail: member@ascd.org
Author guidelines: www.ascd.org/write

Gene R. Carter, *Executive Director;* Nancy Modrak, *Publisher;* Julie Houtz, *Director of Book Editing & Production;* Darcie Russell, *Project Manager;* Greer Beeken, *Graphic Designer;* Mike Kalyan, *Production Manager;* Keith Demmons, *Desktop Publishing Specialist*

All Web links in this book are correct as of the publication date but may have become inactive or otherwise modified since that time. If you notice a deactivated or changed link, please e-mail books@ascd.org with the words "Link Update" in the subject line. In your message, please specify the Web link, the book title, and the page number on which the link appears.

Paperback ISBN: 978-1-4166-0709-0   ASCD product #106035   n9/08
Also available as an e-book through ebrary, netLibrary, and many online booksellers (see Books in Print for the ISBNs).

Quantity discounts for the paperback edition only: 10–49 copies, 10%; 50+ copies, 15%; for 1,000 or more copies, call 800-933-2723, ext. 5634, or 703-575-5634. For desk copies: member@ascd.org.

Library of Congress Cataloging-in-Publication Data

Danielson, Charlotte.
  The handbook for enhancing professional practice : using the framework for teaching in your school / Charlotte Danielson.
     p. cm.
  Includes bibliographical references and index.
  ISBN 978-1-4166-0709-0 (pbk. : alk. paper) 1. Teaching--Handbooks, manuals, etc. 2. Educational planning--Handbooks, manuals, etc. 3. Professional education--Handbooks, manuals, etc. I. Title.

  LB1025.3.D355 2008
  371.102--dc22

                                        2008017349

18 17 16 15 14 13 12 11 10 09 08   1 2 3 4 5 6 7 8 9 10 11 12

The Handbook for *Enhancing* Professional Practice

Using the Framework for Teaching in Your School

Introduction

Since the original publication of *Enhancing Professional Practice: A Framework for Teaching* in 1996, thousands of educators around the world have attested to its value in supporting their examination of practice. This book is intended as a companion volume for educators who have experienced the power of the framework for teaching to shape professional conversation. Educators have found that when their discussions are organized around a clear definition of good teaching, the conversations themselves are more productive and focused than is possible without such a structure.

The most powerful use of the framework for teaching is for teachers' own self-assessment. They locate, often informally, examples from their teaching of the different components of the framework and work to ensure that these reflect increasingly high levels of performance.

In addition, educators have found that the framework for teaching contributes to their work in many different settings and for many different purposes: teacher preparation, the supervision of student teachers, teacher recruitment and hiring, teacher mentoring, peer coaching, professional development, and teacher evaluation. However, to use the framework in all these different ways, educators must have specific procedures and instruments to both structure the conversations and provide guidance for the application of the levels of performance.

A framework for teaching, even when it is organized around a clear and research-based definition of good practice, cannot by itself ensure productive conversations about teaching. Simply having a framework, in other words, is no guarantee of productive and professional interactions among educators. Such interactions depend on *how* the framework is used, the professional culture of the school and the district, the degree of respect among and between teachers and administrators, and the commitment of all educators to ongoing improvement of practice. In particular, if adopted by a school or a district for use in a teacher evaluation system that is governed by a culture of fear, the framework will simply contribute to that culture.

This book, then, is intended to offer practitioners—teachers and their supervisors, mentors, coaches, and others—the tools they need to use the framework for teaching productively in different settings and for different purposes. The tools are designed both to help practitioners examine all aspects of teaching as outlined in the framework in a way that supports the ongoing growth and professional learning of teachers, and to contribute to an overall culture of professional inquiry in a school.

The instruments and protocols offered in this book reflect the combined wisdom of thousands of educators from across the United States and around the world; they represent the best of what has evolved over many years in a range of different settings. It is hoped that the instruments and protocols, with their accompanying recommendations for use, may save practitioners valuable time in developing their own procedures. However, educators should examine them carefully and modify them as necessary to suit conditions in their own schools.

Most of the uses of the framework for teaching—teacher preparation, teacher recruitment and hiring, mentoring and induction, professional development, and performance appraisal—can be clustered into two primary functions: coaching and evaluation. *Coaching* is a nonevaluative process intended to support the development of teaching skill. Teachers and others use it in the following situations:

- Assisting student teachers assigned to their classrooms
- Mentoring colleagues new to the profession
- Providing peers with instruction and guidance

Evaluation involves making judgments about the quality of teaching, and is used for the following purposes:

- Certifying teacher candidates to enter the profession
- Deciding whether to offer tenure or a continuing contract to teachers
- Affirming the continuing skill of experienced teachers
- Determining whether an experienced teacher is performing below standard and should be required to work, under the supervision of an evaluator, on an assistance plan

All of these applications require *evidence* of teaching. To provide feedback to a teacher on performance, it is essential to be specific about that performance, and evidence helps to provide such specificity. The issue of evidence is addressed in Chapter 1.

Whether the primary purpose for using the framework for teaching is coaching or evaluation, all the activities may be used—and *should* be used—to promote professional learning. Such support for learning requires engaging teachers in the thought processes that promote learning—namely, self-assessment, reflection on practice, and professional conversation. These issues are addressed in Chapter 2.

The remaining chapters cover the framework's various specific uses. Teacher preparation, recruitment and hiring, mentoring and induction, coaching, and professional development are addressed in Chapter 3; teacher evaluation is discussed in Chapter 4; and self-directed professional inquiry is covered in Chapter 5. Finally, recommended procedures are outlined in Chapter 6. Instruments and forms to support the procedures and implement the various uses of the framework appear in Appendixes A and B. Regardless of what purpose the framework for teaching is used for or which instruments and procedures are used, readers will find support for two fundamental goals: the evidence-based examination of practice and the professional imperative of promoting teacher learning.

Evidence of Teaching

Meaningful conversations about teaching and valid evaluations of teaching must be grounded in a clear definition of practice—a framework for teaching. This definition should reflect the professional consensus of educators in the particular school or district. Regardless of the purposes to be advanced, whether for professional development or for evaluation of teachers, a clear definition is essential.

But a clear definition of teaching is not sufficient. Both the support of teacher development and the evaluation of teacher performance require *evidence* of practice—evidence of each of the components of teaching identified in the adopted framework. The term *evidence* is not intended to suggest a courtroom or a litigious environment. Rather, it is intended to convey that conversations about teaching must be grounded in actual events, in actions or statements, in artifacts, or in decisions a teacher has made. Without such grounding, impressions of teachers' skills are based entirely on the observers' own idiosyncratic views of teaching and their understandings of what has occurred and what those events mean.

Mentors and coaches, no less than evaluators, depend for their work on evidence of practice. They collect the same evidence but use it for different purposes. For evaluators, evidence is the foundation of judgments they make about teachers. All the evidence they assemble, from a variety of sources—for example, formal and informal observations of practice or artifacts for those aspects of practice not observed in the classroom—serve as the basis of decisions they make about renewing a contract or offering tenure. Mentors and coaches, on the other hand, use the evidence they collect—from the same sources—to structure professional conversations. No judgments are based on it; it is used purely for

1

formative purposes. So the question is not whether individuals in these different roles collect evidence; the question is how they *use* that evidence.

The focus in this chapter is on identifying the evidence needed to describe teachers' skill in the domains and components of teaching described in *Enhancing Professional Practice: A Framework for Teaching*.

Sources of Evidence

Evidence comes from two principal sources: direct observation and the examination of artifacts. Observation is appropriate for the observable aspects of teaching—principally, a teacher's interaction with students in the classroom. But some essential aspects of teaching can't be observed—for example, a teacher's skill in planning or in communicating with families. Although a classroom observation might reveal indirect evidence of, for example, planning, only the planning documents themselves provide a coach or a supervisor with direct evidence of the teacher's skill in designing and sequencing meaningful learning experiences, locating appropriate resources, and developing suitable assessments.

Observation

The observation of classroom practice is the cornerstone of the evidence of a teacher's skill; engaging students in important learning is rightly considered to be the key to professional teaching. What teachers do in their interaction with students is what matters most in influencing student learning.

In general, observation of classroom practice, with the accompanying preconference and postconference, provides the best evidence of Domains 1, 2, and 3 of the framework for teaching: Planning and Preparation, the Classroom Environment, and Instruction. The preconference, also called a planning conference, provides an opportunity for a teacher to display important planning skills, at least as used in planning a single lesson. The postconference, also called a reflection conference, is an important opportunity for teacher self-assessment, reflection on practice, and professional conversation—activities that have been demonstrated to contribute to professional learning by teachers.

Of course, other important aspects of a teacher's work can be observed as well. For example, a teacher's conduct during faculty or team meetings demonstrates the teacher's engagement in a professional community; a parent conference demonstrates the teacher's skill in communicating with families. Furthermore, observations of practice apart from classroom teaching lend themselves to planning and reflection conferences. For example, if a teacher has arranged a presentation to a child study team, the planning conference enables a teacher to respond to questions such as these: "What are you hoping to accomplish?" and "What approach do you plan to take?" Furthermore, the reflection conference may proceed along the same lines as the one following a lesson, with questions such as these: "Did you achieve what you hoped?" "What did you learn from the meeting that causes you to rethink your approach?"

In fact, many educators believe that, from the standpoint of teacher learning, the reflection conference is the most significant part of the observation process, whether the observation has been of a lesson or an event outside the classroom. This has been found to be the case whether the observation has been conducted for purposes of coaching or evaluation. Both the observer and the teacher have witnessed the same events, albeit from different perspectives. That shared experience provides the raw material for meaningful dialogue.

Artifacts

Artifacts offer the best, and in some cases the only, evidence of certain aspects of teaching. The planning documents discussed at the preconference for a lesson observation provide important evidence of a teacher's skill in planning, at least for a single lesson. But what about long-range planning? That is a different and very important skill. Only a unit plan enables teachers to demonstrate how they intend to engage students in sustained learning of complex concepts, with meaningful activities and suitable materials. Through a unit plan, teachers can demonstrate how they develop concepts over time with their students, with the content moving from simpler to more complex, through a variety of approaches. This skill cannot be observed in a single lesson or the lesson plan that accompanies it.

In general, artifacts are essential for teachers to demonstrate their skill in Domains 1 and 4 of the framework for teaching—Planning and Preparation, and Professional Responsibilities. Most of the components of these domains can be observed only indirectly, if at all. No number of classroom observations will enable a teacher to demonstrate the skills of maintaining records, communicating with families, or engaging in professional growth—some of the components of Domain 4. These can best be demonstrated through "stuff"—artifacts. For example, a class newsletter, a phone log, and a letter to parents about a new program indicate the range of a teacher's skill in communicating with families. These written materials should be clear, with proper use of language, and appropriate to the cultural and educational backgrounds of their recipients. For professional conversations or the evaluation of teacher performance in the components of Domains 1 and 4 of the framework for teaching, artifacts are critical.

Artifacts can also provide evidence for Domain 3, Instruction. For example, an assignment or the directions for an activity offer critical evidence of the level of intellectual rigor in the classroom. Furthermore, student work in response to the assignment offers important evidence of student engagement. It's easy to detect whether students have taken the assignment seriously and whether they have engaged thoughtfully with it. Furthermore, in discussing student work with teachers, it's possible to see how they use student work in their informal assessment of student learning.

Figure 1.1 provides some examples across the two dimensions of evidence—direct observation versus examination of artifacts, and classroom practice versus nonclassroom responsibilities. (See Appendix B for guidance on the collection and review of artifacts.)

Figure 1.1
Evidence of Teaching

How to Gather Evidence	Classroom Practice	Nonclassroom Responsibilities
Direct Observation	• Observation of teaching, with a planning conference and a reflection conference	• Observation of practice—for example, a presentation to a child study team or leading a meeting with colleagues
Examine Artifacts	• Analysis of activities and assignments for their cognitive challenge • Analysis of student work	• Planning documents—for example, a unit plan • Examples of components of Domain 4—for example, Communicating with Families

Evidence of Student Learning

The framework for teaching describes the work of teaching. Every component of the framework is supported by empirical research linking the component to increased student achievement. But the framework for teaching is a description of *inputs*—that is, what teachers *do*. As such, it provides only indirect evidence of what is, after all, the main *outcome* of schooling—student learning. Therefore, instead of being asked to demonstrate their skill in teaching, teachers can be asked to provide direct evidence of their results with students. They may be asked to demonstrate that they have actually had an impact on the students they teach.

Evidence of student learning can take many forms. The most obvious form, particularly to noneducators, is the results of state-mandated standardized tests.

State-Mandated Tests and Associated Challenges

State-mandated standardized tests have the advantage of being externally administered and regarded as valid. For the subjects and grade levels in which they are administered, state tests are considered by many people to provide unimpeachable evidence of a teacher's effectiveness. However, the use of state-mandated standardized tests as indicators of a teacher's skill in teaching involves many conceptual and technical difficulties.

Unavailability of state tests for a full range of subjects and levels. State tests are not administered in all subjects and at all grade levels. Most states assess achievement in grades 3 through 8 in math and reading, and sometimes writing and science, and once more in high school, typically in math and reading. For elementary teachers and for middle and high school teachers who teach those subjects, the resulting data can provide an indication, though not a timely one, of their effectiveness. However, state-level tests don't exist for many subjects, or for any actual course at the secondary level—for example, music, world languages, or the sciences such as biology or chemistry. Thus, state-level tests cannot be used to determine the effectiveness of many teachers. For example, even if a state has developed a science test for high school students, such a test will not assess students' knowledge of chemistry.

Incomprehensiveness of state assessments of student learning. Another difficulty with using standardized tests to measure teacher effectiveness is that such tests cannot assess all the learning outcomes considered important by both educators and the general public. For example, multiple-choice, machine-scorable tests can assess student knowledge of facts and procedures, but they are less able to evaluate conceptual understanding, thinking skills, or writing. Furthermore, standardized tests cannot evaluate any aspect of student achievement that depends on student production—for example, giving a presentation or speaking another language.

Student mobility. Any data about student learning is contaminated by the fact that during the course of the year some students enter the school and others leave. These students may not be included in the data, and their exclusion may skew the results. Therefore, the average score of students on a test, particularly if the numbers involved are small, may be highly influenced by the movement in and out of only a few students.

Influences beyond the classroom. Educators and others recognize that student learning—including the learning measured by state-mandated tests—is highly influenced by factors beyond the control of the school. Some families are much better equipped (through their own experiences or the resources they can provide) to support students in their learning. They are able to provide a quiet location for schoolwork and to offer assistance when needed. They can take weekend excursions to local places of interest and provide a home environment that promotes learning. It is well known that such factors greatly influence students' level of performance and rate of learning. Even within the school, student learning cannot always be attributed to individual teachers. Schools are complex systems, and the instructional skill of individual teachers is only one factor, albeit an important one. Other factors that come into play are the curriculum, the school's organization and master schedule, and available learning support. Furthermore, students are sometimes assigned to classes for which they lack important prerequisite knowledge; for example, they may be assigned to an algebra class without having an adequate understanding of fractions.

These various considerations suggest yet another challenge—namely, that test data constitute valid evidence of teaching only if such data are calculated on a value-added rather than an absolute basis; that is, what is the level of proficiency of students at the end of a school year compared with their predicted level of achievement (based on their previous rates of learning)? Such calculations require sophisticated statistical techniques and are possible only where a state or a district has invested heavily in psychometric analysis.

Determining What Is Appropriate Evidence

The challenges related to state-mandated tests are not presented as an argument against asking teachers to demonstrate their impact on the students they teach. Teachers recognize that it is not unreasonable to request that they be able to show that their students learn as a result of their actions. The question becomes one of evidence: How can a teacher demonstrate that? What would count as evidence? How much evidence is sufficient? Could a small sample suffice?

These questions about evidence are most critical in the context of teacher evaluation, where supervisors must be able to say with confidence that a teacher obtains good results with students. The amount and type of evidence of that teacher's impact should be, therefore, decided by the teacher and the supervisor together, and should relate to the school's and the teacher's aims for those students. For example, writing samples from September and May would offer evidence of growth in writing skills, just as science lab reports from fall and spring would demonstrate increased skill in analyzing data. (See Appendix B for guidelines for gathering such evidence.)

Student and Parent Surveys

Some schools and districts encourage the collection and examination of feedback about teacher performance from students and parents. Such feedback can be extremely valuable to teachers in improving their practice. For example, a teacher might strive to treat all students fairly and with respect. But if the students don't believe that all students are treated fairly, the teacher should know that. Similarly, a teacher might strive to be responsive to parent questions and concerns, but if parents find the teacher inaccessible, that is important information for the teacher.

However, collecting information from students and parents presents some challenges. The typical methodology is opinion surveys with a rating scale by which people express their views. By definition, surveys elicit perceptual information—that is, information about people's views and opinions. Such information is not independently verifiable. However, in some instances, perceptions are important. For example, if students believe that a teacher shows favoritism toward some students, it does not matter what the teacher's intentions are or if the "objective" data show something else.

Educators contemplating the use of student and parent surveys must decide whether the respondents will be anonymous. Some students and parents fear retribution if teachers know the source of a negative comment. This retribution could take the form of unpleasant classroom interactions, poor grades, or reluctance by the teacher to write a favorable college recommendation. In addition, it's important to decide what will be done with the results. How will they be used?

Some administrators (and some boards of education) regard the results of student and parent surveys as part of the evaluation process and believe that the results should be sent to the administrator without the teacher even seeing them. In this situation, the issue of respondents' anonymity is not as important. Understandably, most teachers resist this use of student and parent surveys.

In considering the concerns surrounding the evidence that can be derived from student and parent surveys, it seems clear that their primary value is to help teachers understand the impact of their work on the most important people with whom they interact—their students and the parents of those students. Thus it makes sense that teachers be the sole recipients of the feedback, but that they be expected to summarize it to their administrators and be prepared to describe what they have learned from the surveys, what surprises they encountered, and how they plan to address any concerns raised.

Issues Involved in Determining Evidence of Teaching

Many educators collect evidence of teaching for use in several different contexts. Mentors and coaches increase their effectiveness with the teachers they serve if they can cite specific examples of a teacher's practice. And it's essential for evaluators, if they are to make accurate judgments about teaching, to base those judgments on specific evidence of practice. However, a number of issues must be considered in the collection and use of evidence.

Formal Versus Informal Evidence

Evidence—whether gathered through observation of practice or examination of artifacts—may be provided either formally or informally. Most systems of teacher evaluation require a certain number of formal classroom observations, and this requirement is typically spelled out in the negotiated agreement. But *formal* does not necessarily mean "announced"; instead, the term *formal* typically refers to observations that last for a certain minimum length of time, that are documented in a write-up placed in a teacher's file, and that are used in writing the annual evaluation.

An examination of artifacts may be formal as well; the collection of artifacts to be used in, for example, the teacher evaluation may be specified in advance, along with a schedule of when they are to be examined. In some schools, teachers prepare one artifact to be reviewed during the reflection conference for each of the three announced observations. Other schools set aside a separate time for the review of artifacts. In either case, there are no surprises; teachers know what is expected of them, and they have written guidelines to follow.

Most negotiated agreements specify whether evidence gathered informally "counts" in the evaluation process. Some contracts are clear on this point: only evidence collected through the formal (and often announced) observations may be used in making an evaluation. Other contracts include no statement on the point, which means that any evidence, whether it is collected through formal or informal means, may be used.

Announced Versus Unannounced Observations

Another distinction occurs between announced and unannounced observations of practice and examinations of artifacts. Of course, in the context of teacher evaluation, the concept of evidence, and its accuracy, is critical. A strong case can be made for unannounced observations of practice and discussions of artifacts.

How can an administrator know with any certainty the quality of a teacher's practice? Teachers work with students approximately 5 hours each day, for at least 180 days each year, for a total of nearly 1,000 hours. Administrators do well to observe in a teacher's classroom for 4 of those hours each year and may observe for far less than that: typically 1 hour. This is a tiny percentage of the total—well under one-half of 1 percent. The best one can hope for is that the observed lesson is typical, representative of the total. But that conclusion may be unlikely if the observation has been announced; "dog and pony shows" are alive and well! An administrator may witness a lesson that has been much more thoroughly planned than would normally be the case, and for which the students have been specifically prepared.

Administrators sometimes argue that although an announced observation of teaching may cause them to see a highly planned and perhaps not completely typical lesson, it is adequate for their purposes. They can learn, they maintain, whether the teacher is capable of designing and executing a superior lesson.

But surely such an argument is not sufficient. An administrator may determine that a teacher is capable of teaching an excellent lesson when that teacher knows that the administrator will be present. But the students are there every day. To obtain an accurate view of a teacher's practice, it is critical to know, somehow, what happens in the classroom every day, even when no observer is present. This requirement is the strongest argument for including in an evaluation system at least some unannounced observations of teaching. Such observations can be "formal"—that is, they can be for the length of time specified in the contract and can yield a written report, but they are unannounced.

Of course, if a classroom observation is unannounced, it is not possible to conduct a planning conference. As a result, the teacher does not have the same opportunity to demonstrate skill in planning that such a conference affords. However, the planning discussion can be incorporated into the reflection conference—for example, by asking questions such as these: "What were you planning for the students to learn?" "Why were those suitable outcomes for this group of students?"

Unannounced observations of teaching also lend themselves to the unannounced examination of artifacts, particularly those connected to the observed lesson—for example, materials used in the lesson and samples of student work. Other artifacts of a teacher's practice routinely come to the supervisor's attention—for example, information sent to parents or materials prepared for a faculty meeting. Furthermore, teachers' conduct during faculty meetings and team work sessions, their presentation to a child study team, or their sharing of findings from a conference or an action research project are always conducted in the public sphere; observation of these situations is always informal. Figure 1.2 shows some of the characteristics of announced and unannounced and formal and informal procedures for the collection of evidence.

Figure 1.2
Characteristics of Types of Evidence

	Announced	**Unannounced**
Formal	• A classroom observation lasts for at least the minimum time specified in the contract. • Planning conference is included. • Reflection conference is included. • Written lesson summary is included. • Arrangements are made for examination of artifacts. • Results count in teacher evaluation.	• A classroom observation lasts for at least the minimum time specified in the contract. • The observer drops in without previous arrangement. • No planning conference is included. • Written lesson summary is included. • Results count in teacher evaluation.
Informal	• A classroom observation lasts for any length of time. • The teacher knows beforehand that an observer will be coming. • The results *may* count in teacher evaluation.	• A classroom observation lasts for any length of time. • The observer drops in without previous arrangement. • The results *may* count in teacher evaluation.

Collectors and Providers of Evidence

For purposes of mentoring or coaching, teachers collect evidence of the teaching of their colleagues and conduct nonjudgmental conversations about practice. When the evidence is used for performance appraisal, it is typically collected by supervisors or administrators. These may be department chairs, site administrators, or district-level content supervisors. Of course, some exceptions apply; in some settings, teachers are involved in the evaluation of their colleagues. Although rare, this situation is not unknown.

Evidence of teaching may be provided either by the teacher or by a mentor, a coach, or a supervisor. Of course, people's perspectives may differ slightly, because of their different roles. An observer cannot know the background of every situation and can't be aware of the particular challenges facing each individual student. On the other hand, even the most attentive teachers cannot be aware of everything happening in a classroom; another person's observations can help to supplement the teacher's perceptions.

The Importance of Consistency

All educators have a private, idiosyncratic view of good teaching, depending on their own experience as students or as parents with children of school age, their professional preparation, and their experience as teachers and interactions with colleagues. This private vision extends to the type of work students should be doing in school and the nature of suitable communication with families. When teachers join the faculty of a school, their views of teaching may be similar to those of other teachers and supervisors, but not necessarily; the value of an agreed-upon framework for teaching is to provide a common language and a shared understanding for use by teachers and administrators in a school and a district.

But simply adopting the framework for teaching does not guarantee that everyone understands it in the same way or that everyone would cite similar evidence for the different components. To achieve such consistency, training is needed to ensure common understanding of the framework for teaching and, for evaluators, consistent judgments about teaching based on evidence. In addition, the forms and procedures used must support that consistency.

Training to Ensure Consistency

Training in the framework for teaching can be highly valuable professional development for teachers, mentors and coaches, and evaluators. A careful study of *Enhancing Professional Practice: A Framework for Teaching* can provide a good start to becoming familiar with the framework. In such a book study, educators read a chapter of the book between meetings, and they come prepared to discuss the section's applicability to their own setting. For the sections of the book describing the various domains and components, the question of evidence can be added to the discussion: "Does this aspect of teaching apply to me, and if so, what would constitute evidence that it was well done?"

During high-quality training, educators come to understand the different components of the framework for teaching, how the components are related to one another, and which ones share the common themes of, for example, equity, high expectations, or the appropriate use of technology. They learn that the levels of performance in the framework are levels of performance of *teaching*, not of *teachers*, and how evidence is interpreted to reflect those different levels of performance.

But the most valuable aspect of training in the framework for teaching does not consist of the acquisition of skill in assembling evidence for the different components. The greatest value derives from the professional conversations among educators about their practice. In these conversations, teachers acquire ideas from one another ("Oh, that's a good idea; I never thought of doing it that way"), and administrators see the richness of experience that their teachers bring to their work. For this reason, it's important, when possible, for teachers, coaches, and administrators to participate in training together; it's important for teachers not to believe that administrators are engaged in secret activities. For all educators involved in supporting and evaluating teaching, the evidence is the same. Granted, the use to which that evidence is put is different, but the nature of the evidence is identical. And the conversations among all educators are enriched by having in the same room individuals with different perspectives and responsibilities within the school.

Instruments and Forms

Occasionally a school district will announce that it is going to revise its system of teacher evaluation, and then sets about to revise the forms. It's important to recognize that a form is not an evaluation system; the system consists of all its elements, including the evaluative criteria, the procedures, the time lines for activities, and the decisions about who the evaluators are and the training they receive. However, the evaluation instruments (the forms) are important to a good system; they structure the manner in which evaluators collect evidence, and they determine the questions teachers consider for a planning conference and a reflection conference. Similarly, the issues teachers consider in assembling artifacts for a portfolio structure their thinking and their choices. Therefore, the forms provided in Appendixes A and B are offered to stimulate educators' thinking about the types of evidence they want to ask teachers to provide and the nature of the reflection (by teachers, mentors and coaches, and administrators) they intend to encourage.

✳ ✳ ✳ ✳ ✳

When planning for teacher evaluation or designing a system of mentoring, induction, or professional development, evidence of teaching is essential. This is not evidence in a legalistic sense but constitutes the means by which teachers demonstrate their skill. Good teaching is not a mystery; educators, like members of other professions, have developed considerable consensus regarding what constitutes excellent practice. And to ascertain the level of skill, evaluators of teaching must have evidence of that practice. Some of the evidence comes from observations; other evidence comes from artifacts. What is important is that the method used be appropriate to the aspect of practice for which evidence is sought.

Figure 1.3 summarizes the sources of evidence for the components of the framework for teaching. The items in Column 2 refer to forms in Appendix A. The artifacts referred to in Column 5 are described in Appendix B.

Figure 1.3

Sources of Evidence

Domain and Component	Sources of Evidence			
Domain 1 Planning and Preparation	**Teaching, Planning, and Reflection Conferences**	**Observations of Teaching**	**Other Observations of Practice**	**Artifacts**
1a: Demonstrating Knowledge of Content and Pedagogy	Form C: Teaching Interview, Question 1	• Expertise in content		• Unit plan • Activity or assignment
1b: Demonstrating Knowledge of Students	Form C: Teaching Interview, Questions 3, 4; Form F: Planning Conference, Questions 1–8	• Interaction with individual students	• Presentation to a child study team	• Unit plan • Activity or assignment • Communication with families
1c: Setting Instructional Outcomes	Form F: Planning Conference, Questions 1, 2, 4			• Unit plan • Activity or assignment
1d: Demonstrating Knowledge of Resources	Form C: Teaching Interview, Questions 8, 9			• Unit plan
1e: Designing Coherent Instruction	Form F: Planning Conference, Question 5			• Unit plan • Activity or assignment
1f: Designing Student Assessments	Form F: Planning Conference, Question 7			• Unit plan • Activity or assignment
Domain 2 The Classroom Environment	**Teaching, Planning, and Reflection Conferences**	**Observations of Teaching**	**Other Observations of Practice**	**Artifacts**
2a: Creating an Environment of Respect and Rapport	Form C: Teaching Interview, Question 7	• Interactions between teacher and students and among students		
2b: Establishing a Culture for Learning		• Student pride in work • Energy and commitment displayed by the teacher		
2c: Managing Classroom Procedures	Form C: Teaching Interview, Question 5	• Smooth functioning of the classroom		

(continued)

Figure 1.3—*Continued*

Domain and Component	Sources of Evidence			
Domain 2 **The Classroom Environment**	**Teaching, Planning, and Reflection Conferences**	**Observations of Teaching**	**Other Observations of Practice**	**Artifacts**
2d: Managing Student Behavior		• Student conduct • Teacher response to misbehavior		
2e: Organizing Physical Space	Form C: Teaching Interview, Question 10	• Physical space conducive to the lesson		
Domain 3 **Instruction**	**Teaching, Planning, and Reflection Conferences**	**Observations of Teaching**	**Other Observations of Practice**	**Artifacts**
3a: Communicating with Students		• Clarity of teacher directions and explanations		
3b: Using Questioning and Discussion Techniques		• Quality of teacher and student questions and of the discussion		
3c: Engaging Students in Learning		• Quality of student activities • Structure and pacing of the lesson		• Activity or assignment • Samples of student work
3d: Using Assessment in Instruction		• Students receiving feedback • Students engaged in self- and peer assessment • Teacher monitoring of student learning		• Activity or assignment
3e: Demonstrating Flexibility and Responsiveness		• Teacher adjustment when needed • Teacher response to student interests		

| Domain and Component | Sources of Evidence | | | |
Domain 4 Professional Responsibilities	Teaching, Planning, and Reflection Conferences	Observations of Teaching	Other Observations of Practice	Artifacts
4a: Reflecting on Teaching	Form F: Reflection Conference, Questions 1–6; or Form D: Teacher Lesson Reflection			
4b: Maintaining Accurate Records				Instructional and noninstructional records, for example • Record for field trip permissions • Anecdotal notes for student participation
4c: Communicating with Families			• Teacher interaction with parents at school events	Communication with families, for example • Phone log • Samples of weekly newsletter • Handout for back-to-school night • Description of science program
4d: Participating in a Professional Community	Form C: Teaching Interview, Question 13		• Teacher participation in school events • Teacher collaboration with colleagues	Participation in a professional community, for example • Agendas for meetings of the curriculum committee • Log of contributions to the profession • Agendas of meetings of the site council

(continued)

Figure 1.3—*Continued*

Common Themes	Sources of Evidence			
Domain 4 Professional Responsibilities	**Teaching, Planning, and Reflection Conferences**	**Observations of Teaching**	**Other Observations of Practice**	**Artifacts**
4e: Growing and Developing Professionally	Form C: Teaching Interview, Question 2			Professional development, for example • Log of workshops and courses taken • Plan for action research
4f: Showing Professionalism			• Teacher conduct in team and faculty meetings	
Common Themes	**Teaching, Planning, and Reflection Conferences**	**Observations of Teaching**	**Other Observations of Practice**	**Artifacts**
Student Assumption of Responsibility	Form C: Teaching Interview, Question 11			
Appropriate Use of Technology	Form C: Teaching Interview, Question 12			
Attention to Individual Students, Including Those with Special Needs	Form F: Planning Conference, Question 6			

Note: Forms are in Appendix A, artifacts are described in Appendix B.

Promoting Professional Learning

Although the framework for teaching may be used to evaluate teacher performance, its principal contribution to the profession lies in its use in promoting professional learning. It's not the framework itself, of course, that achieves this effect, but the manner in which it is used. Like any tool, it may be misused and applied in a top-down, punitive manner, resulting in a shutting down of teachers' inclinations to engage in learning. Thus, in using the framework for teaching, it's important to recognize those factors that contribute to the desired outcome of promoting professional learning.

A Culture of Professional Inquiry

The first, and in some respects the most important, contributor to professional learning is a culture of inquiry. It is essential that all educators recognize that the work of professional learning never ends; it is a career-long endeavor. When school leaders (both teachers and administrators) insist that it is part of every teacher's responsibility to engage in professional development, this is not to suggest that teachers, either individually or collectively, are deficient in their practice. Rather, it is to maintain that teaching is so complex that it is never done perfectly; every educator can always become more skilled, more expert. And making a commitment to do so is part of the essential work of teaching. It is not an add-on, an extra; rather, it is integral to that work.

Administrators bear a certain responsibility for establishing and maintaining a culture of professional inquiry within a school. Professional learning requires, after all, both time and support. If teachers are to work together to improve their skill, they need to be able to meet together, to observe in one another's class-rooms. This becomes a matter of scheduling and of making professional learning a high priority within the school.

But attitudes matter even more than the details of a school's schedule. A tone of inquiry, one that emphasizes all teachers' obligation to engage in ongoing learning—and the resulting joy in doing so—is essential. Such a tone should infuse daily interactions between teachers and administrators, and among teachers. Educators should come to see their challenges as ones that invite careful analysis of cause, creative solutions, and learning from one another. Improving student learning consists of far more than implementing a new program. Rather, it involves understanding one's students and how they learn and applying the best professional wisdom available. It is also an opportunity to expand that professional wisdom through any available means.

A culture of inquiry, naturally, should infuse a school's practices related to professional development. But this culture can, and should, also be reflected in the school's practices surrounding mentoring and teacher evaluation. When these activities are regarded in the spirit of ongoing learning, they take on an entirely different tone than when they seem to reflect a culture of "gotcha" and uninformed judgment.

Of course, particularly in the area of teacher evaluation, a culture of professional inquiry may represent a considerable departure from past practice. Even experienced teachers may feel anxiety when they see an administrator enter the classroom—even when an outside observer might consider such anxiety to be completely unwarranted. This reaction may be due largely to the fact that teacher evaluation is not being undertaken in an environment of trust (addressed in the next section). But it may also be due to the fact that everyone in the school has traditionally considered teacher evaluation as an exercise to be endured, a necessary fact of life to be accomplished as quickly and painlessly as possible. The idea that even teacher evaluation can be an opportunity for genuine professional learning may be an unfamiliar concept. But teacher evaluation, particularly when it is organized around clearly established and accepted standards of practice, offers an opportunity for educators to reflect seriously on practice; that reflection alone promotes learning. But the culture must support it; it must occur within a culture of inquiry.

Trust

In many schools, a familiar refrain states that a particular practice would be impossible because of a low level of trust. But what does this mean?

In schools, as in other organizations, power is not evenly distributed. Even within a culture of professional inquiry, everyone knows that the buck stops with the administrator. The school principal is held accountable for what happens in the school and is therefore the decision maker of last resort. Even in schools with empowered teacher leaders, department chairs, and instructional coaches, the principal's opinion trumps that of others.

Of course, trust moves up and down the hierarchy; teachers must feel they can trust administrators not to abuse their power, but administrators must believe that they can trust teachers to not undermine the school's mission and reputation. Such development of trust requires honesty and an openness to address issues as they arise. Beyond the matters of honesty and openness, however, the development of trust, particularly from teachers to administrators, rests on a series of important elements described in the following sections.

Professional Competence. First of all, teachers must believe that administrators are knowledgeable and that, therefore, their recommendations are grounded in professional understanding. If teachers are observed by administrators whom they don't believe to be professionally competent, nothing that emerges from the encounter will advance the teachers' learning; the teachers simply won't trust that the administrators know what they are talking about.

Of course, administrators don't have to be experts in every subject or every level to have a deserved reputation for professional competence. But they must be willing to admit the limits of their own knowledge and to be actively engaged in learning from others. And teachers must believe that the administrators know enough to ask the right questions, to bring other insights to bear on a situation, and to advance the collective understanding of everyone involved.

Consistency. Above all, administrators must be consistent in their dealings with teachers; their reaction to a situation must be predictable and stable over time. Otherwise teachers may rightly believe that their encounters with a principal are governed by the whim of the moment or subject to outside pressures. If teachers can't trust a principal to be consistent, they never know where they stand with that individual; before making a proposal, they will be speculating as to the principal's mood.

Furthermore, an administrator's consistency should be grounded in the "big ideas" of the school's vision. In teaching, these ideas are captured in the framework for teaching, which is based on recent research into student learning that maintains that learning is the result of active intellectual engagement by students themselves. Thus, when discussing a lesson, teachers can be confident that they will not be judged according to a vision of classrooms with students sitting quietly at their desks, complying but bored.

Another important element of consistency is transparency. The conversations between teachers and administrators must be based on concepts and beliefs that are publicly known, and the processes must be transparent. Again, in schools that have adopted the framework for teaching as their accepted definition of good teaching, teachers know in advance what constitutes good practice and how their performance will be evaluated. And they must know that their principals have been adequately trained to consistently evaluate that performance based on actual evidence, not on their own idiosyncratic views of teaching.

Confidentiality. Both teachers and administrators must believe that things they say in confidence will stay out of the public eye. This requirement relates to both personal and professional issues and refers to matters both about oneself and about others. Of course, knowledge is power, and some individuals can't resist revealing that they know a particularly "juicy" bit of information. But trusting someone with information requires that anything designated as private must remain so. Violating confidentiality undermines trust as quickly as any other practice.

Admitting Mistakes. Although it may seem a small matter, teachers trust administrators who are willing to admit when they don't have all the answers or, more important, to admit a mistake. It requires a certain largesse and confidence to admit that one was mistaken and that reconsideration of an issue now makes a better response apparent. Admitting mistakes also signals to colleagues that one bases decisions on evidence and analysis, and that as new evidence becomes available, the analysis (and therefore the conclusion) may change.

Sticking with an approach in the face of evidence that it is not effective does not reflect well on the individual. While attempting to appear resolute, to others the person simply looks stubborn. It is one of the hallmarks of professionalism, after all, that the professional stays current about the latest research findings and is prepared to alter practice as a result. Admitting that new evidence has superseded previous advocacy for an instructional approach signals that one is monitoring that evidence and is not afraid to admit that an adjustment should be made. It also signals that if teachers know of an approach they believe is superior to current practice, it will receive serious consideration.

Protecting Against Vulnerability. In the unequal power relationships of schools, teachers' positions—particularly those of nontenured teachers—are insecure. They were hired, of course, in the expectation that they would be able to succeed. But until a teacher has been at work at the school for awhile, no one knows whether the match will turn out to be a good one. Schools are complex places, each with its own culture, and it's difficult to predict whether an individual will fit.

Administrators face an inherent role conflict in their work with nontenured teachers. Most administrators want to be a guide to their new hires, particularly those new to the profession, to help them make a successful transition. But the administrators are also the new teachers' judges, and both parties know it. New teachers are eager to hear positive words from their administrators, to know that they are on the right track. They may be inclined to read significance into small comments made by an administrator, looking for evidence that their performance is being seen as successful.

In this environment, new teachers are vulnerable to the judgment (some would say whim) of the administrator. This is inevitable and is inherent in the situation of administrators evaluating new teachers and having the authority to not renew a contract for little in the way of "cause." A new teacher would have to be brave indeed (or very confident) to seek an administrator's assistance with some students who persist in acting out in class. The teacher has no assurance that such a conversation will not reappear in an annual evaluation as a statement saying "she can't control her class." Unless a high degree of trust has been established (and this is unlikely for new teachers, because they have not yet developed much of a relationship with administrators), teachers won't approach their principals with such concerns.

Administrators can, and most do, work as best they can within the limitations of this situation. They try to assure their new teachers that when they seek assistance the information will not be used against them. They are asking the teachers, in effect, to trust them not to abuse their power, to trust them to protect the teachers' vulnerability.

These considerations account for the importance of a mentoring program, to provide to new teachers an individual with whom they can be completely honest, with whom they can admit their difficulties and seek professional advice. The relationship between a new teacher and a mentor is by its nature nonthreatening, because mentors (except in rare circumstances) don't evaluate teachers. Mentors, in addition to being a resource to new teachers as they are finding their "sea legs," can also serve as coaches to help them prepare for their more formal observations and evaluations conducted by supervisors or principals.

Experienced teachers who have attained tenure can be in a different relationship with their administrators. After all, their attainment of tenure suggests that their performance has been deemed to "meet or exceed" the district's standards of practice. Hence, unless otherwise indicated, their positions are secure; their interactions with administrators are situated within a different professional milieu than are those of nontenured teachers. The conversations can be far more collegial and more collaborative for the simple reason that the teachers themselves are not as vulnerable.

Overall, working in a trusting environment means that people feel safe, secure that others are telling the truth; that it is safe to admit vulnerabilities and that others aren't asserting their power as a substitute for rational discussion. A trusting environment is an open environment, where issues are on the table and teachers are not made to feel more vulnerable than absolutely necessary.

Self-Assessment and Reflection on Practice

As philosophers since ancient times have noted, self-knowledge is the beginning of wisdom. Teachers' awareness of their own areas of strength and need for growth is the first step toward professional improvement. Teaching is highly complex and demanding work; for many teachers (particularly new teachers) simply making it through the day is a tall order.

But making it through the day is not sufficient to strengthen practice. And although it appears that we learn from our actions, that view is not quite accurate. It's not that we learn from our actions; we learn from our *thinking* about our actions. It's the thinking that matters. Hence, to acquire the capacity to improve their teaching, teachers must be able to analyze it, to recognize their areas of relative strength and weakness.

Naturally, clear standards of practice help in the process of self-assessment. When many teachers first encounter the framework for teaching, they examine the rubrics to determine where their own teaching falls in the levels of performance. Doing this privately enables them to be honest in their assessment. Then, for many of them, their eyes drift to the right, to see what performance at the next higher level would be. For many teachers, their response is "Oh, sure, I can do *that*." That is, the framework for teaching becomes a tool for an individual examination of practice that will lead in the future to modest changes.

Reflection on practice requires both skill and discipline. Beginning teachers, before they have acquired the skill of reflection, tend to report that a lesson was "fine" or "terrible," global judgments that don't represent the nuances of the situation. Only with experience, and aided by structured support from a mentor, a coach, or even an administrator, do novice teachers look beneath the surface and explore more complex questions about their teaching. At that point, when invited to do so, they are able to consider whether the instructional outcomes they set for their students were appropriate, whether students were engaged in productive learning, whether the student groups should have been formed differently, or whether the learning activities were productive. By analyzing a lesson one element at a time, teachers become more analytical, more reflective, and more evidence-based in their thinking. Such thinking then becomes a habit of mind that teachers engage in independently on a regular basis.

Even when the habit is well established, however, reflection on practice requires both time and discipline. Immediately following a lesson is the best time to think about it and to determine how it could have been improved. But most teachers must move from one lesson to another immediately; even at the end of the day their attention is focused on preparations for the following day. In addition to the time required to "replay the tape" of a lesson just completed, teachers need to value the practice sufficiently to apply the discipline required.

Naturally, as teachers gain experience with self-assessment and reflection on practice, it is easier to do and requires less time. Teachers can mentally run through the different elements of the lesson—the instructional goals, the activities, and the manner in which the students have been grouped—and ask themselves the fundamental reflection question: "If I had a chance to teach this lesson again, what would I do differently?" Then, while the answer is fresh in their minds, they can make quick notes to review before teaching it again.

The procedures and instruments in this book are designed to support teacher self-assessment and reflection on practice. They invite teachers to consider a lesson, for example, in light of the domains and components of the framework for teaching, and to identify evidence, as appropriate, of those components. This self-assessment and reflection on practice become, then, the foundation for conversation with other educators regarding the lesson and the first step toward strengthening practice.

Collaboration and Conversation

In their purest forms, self-assessment and reflection on practice can be done by teachers on their own, thinking through lessons they have taught or parent conferences they have conducted for insight on how they could have been done better. Initially, that is, self-assessment and reflection on practice are independent activities. However, there are limits as to what one can discover on one's own; perceptive questions from another educator can stimulate thought in new directions and lead to new discoveries.

Furthermore, self-directed professional inquiry (described in Chapter 5) ideally includes a process in which teachers work with colleagues, in study groups if possible, to explore an important aspect of practice or to engage in action research. The collaborative aspect of such projects is important; multiple participants enable the expression of multiple perspectives. Different educators focus on different aspects of the same situation and bring their own experience to bear. These multiple angles can only enrich the quality of what emerges.

When watching a videotape of a class, for example, or when observing a live lesson, observers will see things the teacher was unaware of while the lesson was unfolding. Such different perspectives contribute to the teacher's awareness of a situation, of course. But the collaboration accomplishes something else as well: everyone in the group learns from the exercise. If a teacher has brought a situation to a study group to be discussed and resolved, the teacher benefits from the perspectives of everyone in the group. But the other members of the group learn as well; they become aware of a new professional situation, and they hear the views of their colleagues. Collaboration and discussion benefits everyone in the group.

Naturally the mechanism through which such learning occurs is conversation. Whether it is in a study group, or one-on-one with a coach or supervisor, conversation is the mechanism through which thoughts are expressed. The English language even has idioms that point out the close connection between thought and speech, as in "I'm just thinking out loud here," or "How do I know what I think until I hear myself say it?" Conversation, one could argue, is thought made accessible. Thus a principal vehicle for promoting learning is collaboration and conversation, because educators must explore their thinking, express it to others, and learn from the perspectives of others.

✳ ✳ ✳ ✳ ✳

The principal value of the framework for teaching is in promoting professional learning by teachers and other educators. It provides a tool for them to arrive at consensus, first of all, as to what constitutes good teaching. Then, in using this tool for a variety of purposes—teacher preparation, mentoring and coaching, professional development, and teacher evaluation—educators can adopt procedures that emphasize the learning (rather than the inspection) aspect of those activities.

Any framework for teaching could yield such benefits; the actual tool is not particularly important so long as it is grounded in solid research. The key to promoting professional learning lies in the procedures adopted and the culture within which the framework is used. In a punitive environment, no framework for teaching, regardless of its merits, will ensure professional growth.

When conducted within a culture of inquiry, however, conversations based on the framework for teaching offer a rich opportunity for professional learning. The instruments and procedures provided in this book are designed to support such learning.

Using the Framework Across the Career Spectrum

3

A notable feature of the framework for teaching is its usefulness for educators in various roles—teacher trainers, teachers, and school and district administrators. In addition, the framework's usefulness spans all phases of a career in education, from the preparatory years through the years spent honing the skills and knowledge that qualify one as an outstanding practitioner. This chapter describes how best to use the framework for teacher preparation, recruitment and hiring, mentoring and induction, and coaching and professional development. Appendix A contains the various forms referred to in the following sections.

Teacher Preparation

Teacher educators face the daunting challenge of preparing their students for a highly complex profession, with limited time for doing so. Even in a five-year, or master's, program, time is short. Therefore, teacher preparation programs, like education at all levels, must be highly purposeful and organized efficiently around clear outcomes. A teacher education program should be able to clearly specify what it expects its graduates to know and be able to do, and how it will verify that they have achieved those aims.

Teacher educators have found the framework for teaching to be a useful organizing structure for their programs. If the framework represents good teaching, the argument goes, are we teaching our candidates the skills delineated in the framework? Are they aware of these concepts and ideas? Can they design instruction to ensure student engagement?

Of course, the framework for teaching may influence several aspects of the preparation program, including the actual course offerings and the clinical experience of students (both their own student teaching and their observations of classroom teachers). Thus the framework can help to ensure that all graduates of a program are fully equipped to succeed as the teacher of record in a classroom. In addition, it can be used to certify their skill.

Course Content

Course offerings for teachers-in-training must include a wide range of topics and perspectives. It is important for those entering the profession to have a broad awareness of the history and mission of education, the place of education in a democratic society, and the history of how the role of education has evolved over time. Not all of these aspects of teaching are addressed directly in the framework for teaching, although they underlie 21st century practice. Foundational work—that is, theories and the knowledge gained from applications of those theories over time—is, after all, the foundation for current practice. As the popular expression puts it, "There is nothing as practical as a good theory."

In addition, of course, new teachers must enter the field equipped to meet the practical challenges of everyday classroom life, which have been described in detail in *Enhancing Professional Practice: A Framework for Teaching* (Danielson, 2006). These challenges are complex and may be daunting to those entering the profession. A program that prepares teachers must at least enable them to be successful as they embark on their careers; the courses teachers-in-training take should teach them practical skills as well as provide a theoretical perspective.

How can a preparation program ensure that its students acquire the important knowledge and skill they need to be successful? That is where the framework for teaching has proved to be useful: teacher educators can conduct an audit of a program's course offerings that deal directly with practice, to ensure that the important aspects of teaching described in the framework are included in the syllabi for the various courses, and that student understanding of the necessary knowledge and skill is assessed through course examinations and practical demonstrations.

In conducting an audit, most preparation programs will discover that everything in their syllabi is, in fact, important in the framework for teaching. Indeed, many courses in classroom management or methods of instruction in the various disciplines and levels directly include the issues described in Domain 1, Planning and Preparation; Domain 2, The Classroom Environment; and Domain 3, Instruction. And to the extent that a preparation program also includes the skills of communicating with families, it may also prepare teachers for at least some of the aspects of Domain 4, Professional Responsibilities. In many preparation programs, courses are designed to address a specific aspect of the framework for teaching—for example, the content and pedagogical techniques in the disciplines (Component 1a), how to establish smooth routines and procedures (Component 2c), and how to create a student-centered approach to student discipline (Component 2d).

In addition, the common themes described in Chapter 3 of *Enhancing Professional Practice: A Framework for Teaching* can offer another important lens through which to view the preparation of teachers. The themes are the following:

- Equity
- Cultural competence
- High expectations
- Developmental appropriateness
- Attention to individual students, including those with special needs
- Appropriate use of technology
- Student assumption of responsibility

In fact, several of the themes can provide the focus for courses on, for example, cognitive and emotional development, the impact of cultural differences on the challenges of planning, differentiation for individual student needs, and the use of technology in planning and teaching. The insights from these courses can then provide important perspectives on the actual work of teaching in different settings, designing instruction, engaging students in learning, assessing student work, and the like.

Form A: *Teacher Preparation Audit* can be used to examine a preparation program and to identify where there are holes that should be filled through additions or revisions to the program.

Clinical Practice

Through time spent in schools and classrooms, teachers-in-training acquire essential first-hand experience using the knowledge and skills they have learned in their coursework. Initially they are observers and interviewers of experienced teachers; later they apply what they have learned in teaching lessons on their own.

Observations of experienced teachers. Typically the first field experience of teachers-in-training is observing experienced teachers, often in a wide range of settings. Unless they make a special effort, however, their first experience tends to be somewhat unfocused; they are asked to simply observe teachers and summarize what they have seen.

The framework for teaching provides a structure for these observations. Teachers-in-training will, after all, have been learning about the domains and components of the framework; what better way to understand them more deeply than to observe an experienced teacher and see them in practice? In observing experienced teachers, teachers-in-training not only see how the domains and components play out in different settings. They can actually see evidence of how teachers manage to implement them.

Form B: *Clinical Observation Notes* may be used to document such observations. It lists each of the domains and components that might be observed in a class and summarizes the main points of each. It then provides a space where teachers-in-training may jot notes of how each of the components has been demonstrated in the class they observed—for example, what the teacher did or said, what the students did or said, or how the room was arranged. Of course, depending on the lesson, the teacher-in-training may see no evidence at all for one or more of the components; in that case, the space should simply be left blank.

Back in class at the university, teachers-in-training can discuss the techniques they have observed. They can compare notes on how different teachers established, for example, environments of respect in their classrooms, or the methods they used to encourage students to take an active role in class discussions. By focusing their observations in this manner and by discussing them with their professors and fellow students, teachers-in-training derive maximum benefit from the time they spend in schools building their own repertoire of skills that they will later use.

Interviews of experienced teachers. Another important source of information and insight for teachers-in-training is interviews with experienced teachers. It's one thing to observe an experienced teacher in action; it's quite another thing to ask teachers how, for example, they plan lessons, ensure that all students are engaged, or encourage students to take responsibility for their own learning.

Advanced skills of teaching may not be obvious to an inexperienced observer. The teacher-in-training might accurately observe, for example, that the students in a class know exactly what to do when the teacher announces that they should move into their groups for an activity. But how did the teacher prepare them for this? How did the teacher teach them what to do so that the environment is not chaotic? To the inexperienced eye, highly accomplished teaching might look like magic; it might seem that the class is running itself. By interviewing the teacher, the teacher-in-training pulls back the curtain on the teacher's thinking and is able to understand how the experienced teacher creates the class that was observed.

Form C: *Teaching Interview* can serve as a starting point for these important conversations, for learning about an experienced teacher's approaches and techniques. In these conversations, teachers explain the thinking behind the decisions that inform their practice. In responding to the questions, they reveal their teaching as a series of deliberate, purposeful judgments influenced by multiple aspects of context. (Appendix A provides two versions of Form C. The annotated version explains the framework components each interview question is designed to illuminate and can help teachers-in-training focus the conversation.)

Student teaching. When teachers-in-training begin their own student teaching, the framework is a valuable tool both for their own self-assessment and for informal observations of their teaching by a cooperating teacher. For self-assessment, Form D: *Teacher Lesson Reflection* is the most suitable form; it asks student teachers to consider a lesson they have taught in light of the components in Domains 1, 2, and 3 of the framework for teaching. Of course, depending on the lesson, there may be no evidence for some of the components.

Student teachers, their cooperating teachers, and their supervisors should all be aware of expectations regarding the practice of student teachers. As described in *Enhancing Professional Practice: A Framework for Teaching*, the rubrics represent levels of performance of *teaching*, not of *teachers*. As such, they reflect teachers' knowledge and experience with different disciplines and students of different ages. "Unsatisfactory" performance represents practice that is beneath the licensing standard of "do no harm": harm is being done, or learning is being shut down, or the environment is chaotic. "Basic" performance reflects typical performance of teachers new to the profession, individuals who are doing virtually everything for the first time. Therefore, the Basic level is appropriate for the performance of both student teachers and teachers in their first year or two of practice. When teachers are first acquiring experience, their performance is inconsistent; they probably don't have a Plan B, and they may not yet recognize the signs of a lesson requiring adjustment while it is underway. "Proficient" and "Distinguished" teaching are characteristic of experienced educators, those who have developed their routines, who consistently engage students in high-level learning, and whose students assume considerable responsibility for the success of the class. In particular, Distinguished performance reflects highly accomplished teaching, a level that a novice teacher would rarely attain.

As student teachers gradually assume responsibility for a classroom, their cooperating teachers have many opportunities to observe their performance informally and to provide feedback. Form E: *Informal Classroom Observations* provides a convenient instrument for collecting the results of multiple observations. It includes two components from Domain 1 (1a: Demonstrating Knowledge of Content and Pedagogy, and 1b: Demonstrating Knowledge of Students) that, to a far greater extent than the other components in Domain 1, are likely to be demonstrated in classroom practice as well as through conferences. All the components of Domains 2 and 3 are also included, as they are consistently demonstrated in a classroom observation. However, in any given lesson, particularly a brief one, it's likely that only some of the components would be on display.

In using Form E, each time cooperating teachers observe student teachers, even briefly, they note the date and the concept being taught on the first page. Then, as they see evidence of the different components of teaching, they write that evidence in the space below the appropriate component. If a clear level of performance has been demonstrated by that evidence, they can indicate that level with a highlighter. A refinement of this practice is to indicate each informal observation with a different color of highlighter. Then, over the course of several months of conducting informal observations, the teacher's increasing level of skill is evident in a strikingly visual manner.

In virtually all programs, supervisors from the university visit the student teachers and observe a complete lesson, with a planning conference and a reflection conference. In some programs, cooperating teachers are asked to conduct formal observations of student teachers, with the results contributing to the student teachers' evaluations. Any educators asked to judge the performance of student teachers, whether they are university supervisors or cooperating teachers, must be trained sufficiently for their role so they can make valid and consistent judgments based on evidence of practice. Successful completion of student teaching is a high-stakes matter for the student; it's essential that the people making those judgments be able to make them well. This ability is a matter of training—training in the framework for teaching, in observation skills, and in the collection and interpretation of evidence. Such training is typically offered through the university program, although it might also be offered by a school district for its own administrators, mentors, and teachers.

Cooperating teachers and supervisors may use the Notes section of Form F: *Formal Classroom Observation* to take notes during a class. Using the left-hand column to write down the time an event occurred permits later analysis of the lesson for issues of pacing and balance. Then, following the lesson, the cooperating teacher or supervisor should consider each of the items noted from the lesson and determine the component of the framework for teaching represented by each one. The component number (such as *2a* or *3b*) may be written in the right-hand column.

The observer may then analyze the notes according to the components in the framework for teaching, using Form G: *Formal Observation Summary.* As with the informal observation notes (Form E), the observer should write evidence for each component of the framework in the space below the rubric for that component and then determine the level of performance. This is a far more powerful exercise if the student teacher also reflects on the lesson, using Form D: *Teacher Lesson Reflection.* When the student teacher and the supervisor compare their perceptions of the lesson, the conversation is exceedingly rich and can isolate aspects of teaching that should be strengthened. The items on the final page of Form G (areas of strength and areas for growth) are best completed jointly. Thus the observation form provides a structure for the observation, feedback, and assessment of progress.

Of course, the observation instruments may need to be modified slightly to reflect the work of student teachers. Student teachers, after all, are not the teacher of record; they inherit and gradually assume responsibility of the class of an experienced teacher—one who has established the routines and procedures, the standards of classroom conduct, and the patterns of interactions among students. The degree of success in these matters is not entirely—or even primarily—the consequence of the student teacher's work. Even the quality of the lesson design, or modifications made for individual students, may represent the combined work of the student teacher and the cooperating teacher.

But with these reservations in mind, the observation instruments are extremely valuable in structuring the cooperating teachers' and supervisors' observations of student teachers, and the interview protocols structure the conversations before and after the observation to maximize reflection on practice. See Figure 3.1 for a list of the forms that are useful for teacher preparation programs.

Figure 3.1
Forms for Teacher Preparation

Form A: *Teacher Preparation Audit*—For teacher-training institutions to use to examine their programs and determine the need for additions or revisions

Form B: *Clinical Observation Notes*—For teachers-in-training to use when observing experienced teachers

Form C: *Teaching Interview*—For teachers-in-training to use in interviewing experienced teachers

Form D: *Teacher Lesson Reflection*—For teachers-in-training to use in analyzing their own practice

Form E: *Informal Classroom Observations*—For cooperating teachers to use in providing feedback from informal observations

Form F: *Formal Classroom Observation*—For cooperating teachers or university supervisors to use to structure a planning conference, an observation, and a reflection conference

Form G: *Formal Observation Summary*—For cooperating teachers or university supervisors to use during a reflection conference, to provide structured feedback on a formal observation

Recruitment and Hiring

The challenge faced by schools and districts in hiring new teachers is to ensure that they make good decisions, that the teachers they hire not only will excel in the classroom with students but also will be able to contribute to the school's professional community. The challenge is particularly great when considering teachers new to the profession, because it is not possible to contact previous employers or to send interviewers to observe the teachers in their own classroom.

However, even with the challenges, the framework for teaching can provide a structure for the selection process that would not be possible without such a tool. It ensures that a consistent definition of good teaching is applied to all candidates, both making the process more transparent and making favoritism in hiring less likely.

It is important that hiring decisions be informed by the perspectives of both teachers and administrators. Teachers are keenly aware of the issues confronting their own schools (and departments or teams within those schools) and therefore the skills needed in prospective colleagues. Thus the selection process for teachers new to a school should include, whenever possible, participation by both teachers and administrators, at least in the final stages.

A well-designed recruitment and hiring process bases hiring decisions on evidence from a number of sources: review of résumés, interviews with candidates, observation of actual teaching or examination of a videotape (for experienced teachers), and review of artifacts (such as planning documents and class newsletters). These are each discussed separately in the sections that follow.

Review of Résumés

Résumés present teachers' descriptions of what they regard as most relevant to a particular vacancy or type of vacancy, such as elementary teacher or secondary teacher of mathematics. They summarize previous teaching posts, noting the important responsibilities of the position, the students served, and important characteristics of the community. In addition, most teachers will include nonteaching activities in which they participated, such as service on school or district committees, supervision of student activities, or outreach to parents or the business community.

Of course, candidates who are new to the profession will not be able to include teaching positions on their résumés, although as young people they might have worked in positions such as swimming teacher or camp counselor. Teachers who have been part of a traditional teacher preparation program will be able to include salient details of that program on their résumés, including the courses they have taken and their field placements. But teachers entering the profession through an alternate route may not have such details available. However, many such candidates will be able to offer alternate, and sometimes highly relevant, experience, such as working with young people as a scout master or an athletic coach, or as teacher in a church or a synagogue. Many alternate-route candidates are older than traditional candidates, with important life experience, such as parenting or working in an organization.

In reviewing résumés, educators should bear in mind the skills and disposition they are seeking and maintain an open mind about how an individual may have acquired such skills. Naturally, reading résumés is only the first level of screening of candidates, but it's important that those doing the screening don't hold an overly rigid view of what is acceptable.

Interviews

Naturally, interviews with candidates are critical in establishing a personal connection and determining whether a candidate is a good fit with the school's culture and approach to instruction. It is now well accepted that teaching is a complex cognitive activity and that teachers make hundreds (literally—researchers have counted them) of decisions each day. Thus it's not sufficient to observe what teachers *do*; it's also important to understand the thinking behind their decisions. Interviews provide a window into teachers' thinking, enabling them to explain their reasoning and their rationale for decision making.

It's also important to standardize the interview process so that those conducting the interviews obtain responses to the same questions from all candidates for a position. Of course, schools and districts will have questions to put to candidates that reflect that particular setting. But to the extent that educators seek candidates' responses to questions directly related to the framework for teaching, they will find the questions on Form C: *Teaching Interview* useful. These questions are designed to elicit candidates' skills and experience with respect to many components of the framework for teaching. Some of these components, such as those related to routines and procedures, may be observed in a classroom or on a videotape. But the interview reveals the teacher's thinking behind the routines established and enables the teacher to describe, for example, the techniques used to encourage students to participate in the establishment of those routines.

Observation

Direct observation of teachers' skill with students is an important aspect of determining the suitability of a candidate for a teaching position. Many teachers can talk about their teaching in an engaging manner, describing what sounds, to the listener, like imaginative, student-centered practice. However, the description may be very different from what they display when interacting with students, when actually teaching a lesson. Only an observation of actual practice can enable those making the hiring decision to determine the candidate's true skill.

A teacher's skill with students may be demonstrated by three methods:

• Having the candidate teach a lesson to a group of students at the site with the vacant position (students whom the candidate has not met before the lesson)

• Sending an observer to watch the candidate conduct a lesson with her own class

• Asking the candidate to submit a video of her teaching, with students in her current class

Each of the first two methods has advantages and disadvantages. Clearly, teaching a lesson to unfamiliar students is an artificial situation; the teacher has not had the opportunity to establish a relationship with them, and they may not be displaying their typical behavior. However, it does provide "live" evidence without the inconvenience of an observer traveling to the candidate's own school. And for candidates who are not currently teaching (or who are new to the profession), it may be the only way to see them in action. Sending an observer to watch a candidate teach at the candidate's own site certainly provides the most accurate picture of that person's skill. The lesson is likely to be authentic, and it's possible to see the teacher with students who are familiar with the teacher's routines and general approach. Of course, all the limitations of formal observations used for evaluation are evident in this situation as well; teachers can put on a good show that may inflate their actual skill. And the lesson may have been meticulously organized, with no deviation from the plan; hence the observer may not have the opportunity to see how a teacher responds to unexpected events.

The last method, asking candidates to submit a videotape of their teaching, also has a number of disadvantages. First, the quality of the tape may be poor, particularly if the teacher is inexperienced in making videotapes. If the camera was set up facing a window, for example, everyone may be in shadow. Second, unless the teacher has taken special care, it likely won't be easy to hear the students—and possibly the teacher—speak. Lastly, the teacher may have edited the tape, cutting out parts that might give an unfavorable impression.

However, despite the disadvantages, a videotape of classroom teaching also offers important advantages in the selection process. First, the tape may be watched by many different observers (for example, the entire interview team), and they can watch it more than once. In addition, during an interview the tape may be played, paused at important points in the lesson, and the teacher asked to describe what was happening, how the lesson built on earlier learning experiences, or the characteristics of individual students. The tape represents, in other words, significant raw material for understanding a teacher's practice.

Interviewers can use the observation instruments (Forms F and G) to organize their observations of either a sample lesson the candidate teaches as part of the selection process or a videotape submitted by the candidate. Form F: *Formal Classroom Observation* provides a template for note taking, with space in the left-hand column to indicate the time of different events. Then the interviewer can code each item in the notes to different components of the framework for teaching, writing those components in the right-hand column. The evidence of practice for each of the components then may be transferred to the appropriate section of Form G: *Formal Observation Summary* and interpreted against the levels of performance.

Use of such instruments allows the observations of different individuals to be consistent and the subsequent decisions to be grounded in concrete evidence of practice. Of course, if the lesson is taught to students who are new to the candidate, that context must be taken into account in how the observation notes are interpreted against the levels of performance.

Examination of Artifacts

The most dynamic illustration of a teacher's skill is, of course, in that teacher's work with students in a classroom setting. But teaching involves much behind-the-scenes work—for example, unit and lesson planning. In addition, conversations with a teacher, especially with samples of student work as a stimulus for discussion, reveal much about the teacher's thinking. Furthermore, many important aspects of a teacher's work simply don't occur in the classroom at all (for example, communicating with families or working with colleagues). For educators to make an informed decision about a prospective teacher's skill, it's important to see evidence of these nonclassroom responsibilities.

Compiling a professional portfolio can be a valuable experience for new and prospective teachers. Determining what should go in the portfolio requires collecting artifacts, comparing possible entries, and selecting the best or the one that best represents some aspect of practice. This process is valuable for the person doing it, in that it requires focused reflection and decision making, as well as judgments on quality. For experienced teachers applying for a new job, documenting their work outside the classroom results in reflection on practice and can lead to new insights into their teaching.

Assembling artifacts may not be a new experience for teachers. As part of many teacher preparation programs, students compile an extensive portfolio of their approach to teaching and use it in presenting themselves to prospective employers. Some of these are elaborate affairs, with photographs of their student-teaching classrooms and testimonials from students and colleagues.

When considering a candidate for a teaching position, it's important for a school or district to be purposeful and specific. More is not necessarily better. Portfolios compiled as part of a teacher preparation program may represent more than what is needed (or even desired) by an interview team; many portfolios are overkill. But the team can establish some guidelines themselves as to what candidates are asked to submit as part of their application.

In deciding what to ask teachers new to the profession to provide, the decision should be governed by three principles. First, the request should not be overwhelming, requiring many hours of preparation. Second, the artifacts should be those that can reasonably be expected of a teacher who is not currently teaching or who has completed only student teaching. Lastly, the artifacts should be selected deliberately to provide the selection committee with evidence of aspects of a teacher's practice that can be derived only through such artifacts. Therefore, a selection of artifacts that might reasonably be requested of teacher candidates new to the profession could include the following:

- A unit plan, with its assessment
- A lesson plan, with the questions on the planning protocol from Form F answered in writing
- An instructional artifact, including student work if the artifact had actually been used with students

Candidates with experience in another school or district can base their collection of artifacts on actual teaching, and their choice of documents can reflect their experience. These could include artifacts to illustrate the following:

- Analyzing student work using an instructional artifact
- Communicating with families
- Participating in a professional community
- Engaging in professional growth

It's important to recognize that although the principal value of artifacts in the process of recruitment and hiring is to enable candidates to demonstrate their skill in the different components of the framework, a critical part of that hiring process consists of the conversations about the artifacts. Discussion questions can prompt important teacher reflection and provide the foundation for conversations that reveal the nature of teachers' thinking about their practice. (Appendix B contains guidelines for preparing artifacts.)

A Signal to Newly Hired Teachers

Some districts give newly hired teachers a copy of the book *Enhancing Professional Practice: A Framework for Teaching*. This gesture offers a public declaration of what the district values in good teaching. Such an act announces to new staff that teaching well is the highest priority and that the district has devoted serious thought to defining good teaching. Using the framework in both the recruiting and hiring processes signals that the district's definition of good teaching is clear and that such a definition constitutes the foundation of other elements of the district's human resources policy: mentoring and induction, professional development, and teacher evaluation. See Figure 3.2 for a list of forms that are useful in teacher recruitment and hiring.

Figure 3.2

Forms for Teacher Recruitment and Hiring

Form C: *Teaching Interview*—For recruiters to use in interviewing teacher candidates

Form F: *Formal Classroom Observation*—For recruiters to use in observing live or taped lessons taught by a candidate

Form G: *Formal Observation Summary*—For recruiters to use in analyzing the strengths of a lesson by a candidate

Mentoring and Induction

Most educators recognize that learning to teach extends into the first several years of teaching: Regardless of the quality of a teacher preparation program, important skills cannot be learned until an individual is the teacher of record. Furthermore, much of teaching becomes better with practice and through familiarity with the school environment.

Teaching is virtually the only profession without a built-in apprenticeship. Apprenticeship is institutionalized in medicine with the internship and the residency. Airline pilots fly with more experienced and trained instructors before they are permitted to fly solo. Architects and accountants work under the supervision of more experienced colleagues before they are assigned their own clients. Other professions, in other words, are structured such that those new to the field are not left to survive on their own, to "sink or swim." Professions other than teaching are structured to ensure the success of those new to the profession.

Regrettably, the job of teaching for the 10-year veteran is exactly the same as it is for the novice; indeed, the assignment of the novice may actually be more demanding—working from a cart instead of being assigned to a single classroom, having the highest number of course preparations, and working with some of the school's most challenging students. Furthermore, new teachers are doing everything for the first time, and classroom events rarely proceed completely according to plan, even for experienced teachers. But whereas experienced teachers have an extensive repertoire and a broader awareness of what to expect, new teachers are frequently caught with a need to make adjustments even though they have not prepared a Plan B. All this adds to the stress of learning to teach, making the availability of a mentor that much more valuable. It is small wonder that the rates of attrition for teachers are high, resulting in disillusionment on the part of the teachers and instability in the school.

Mentoring and induction of new teachers, then, is an important responsibility for schools and districts to undertake. The results of well-designed programs are impressive, for example, with the retention rate for new teachers supported by the New Teacher Center of Santa Cruz, California, approaching 95 percent. Such programs combine practical support (how to find materials and supplies, how to conduct a parent conference) with formative assessment of new teachers by mentors, and feedback on teaching. The programs engage the new teachers in self-assessment, reflection on practice, and professional conversations—activities that contribute to professional learning.

Many schools have had mentoring programs for some time, typically using "buddies" to help new teachers navigate the systems for ordering supplies, gaining access to professional resources, and the like. They also help new teachers understand the school's culture for such things as back-to-school night and parent conferences. But although such traditional mentoring programs include needed emotional support for new teachers, they are rarely more than a buddy system. Important as such support is, it is not sufficient; knowing the school's culture for back-to-school night and parent conferences is important, but so is skill building in those areas. That is, new teachers may need guidance on how to conduct a parent conference, regardless of the culture in a particular school. And new teachers are still refining their teaching skills and consolidating their craft. Such refinement requires instructional-based coaching.

New Teachers Learning from Experienced Teachers

One important activity for beginning teachers is to interview teachers who are more experienced. New teachers can gain insights into the thinking of their more experienced colleagues—thinking that shapes the results in their classrooms. Questions from Form C: *Teaching Interview* can structure these conversations, which are best conducted after school, when neither teacher is responding to students or assembling materials for a class that's about to begin.

In addition, new teachers can benefit from watching experienced teachers in action. The proof of teachers' planning and preparation is, after all, in how they use their skill in working with students. Such observations of experienced teachers are most productive if they are focused on certain specific aspects of practice, such as organizing classroom routines or conducting discussions in which students take on a leadership role. Form B: *Clinical Observation Notes* may be useful in conducting these observations. Alternatively, the conversations can take place using no established forms at all. However, taking notes on the conversations is advisable because it's easy to forget what was said, and it's helpful for a beginning teacher to be able to look up the comments later, when the need arises.

Mentors Observing Beginning Teachers

Mentors can be extremely useful to beginning teachers by observing them in the classroom and providing feedback on their performance. These observations may be informal, to provide the raw material for conversation; or they may be more formal, to help prepare a teacher for observations that may be used for teacher evaluation. Depending on the situation, mentors can use Form E: *Informal Classroom Observations*, Form F: *Formal Classroom Observation*, and Form G: *Formal Observation Summary* to structure their activity.

It is essential for mentors to be trained for their role in the skills of observation, structuring feedback, and conducting reflective conversations. These are not skills that most teachers will have acquired during their own teacher preparation. Even highly experienced and skilled teachers, then, need to be prepared for the role of assisting in new teachers' learning.

Training for mentors should consist of understanding the standards of practice (the framework for teaching) as well as coaching skills designed to enhance the work of new teachers. Of course, the value of such training, and of the mentoring program itself, is not confined to the new teachers. Many mentors report that their own teaching has improved as a result of observation skills, collecting and interpreting evidence against clear standards of teaching, and both providing feedback and engaging new teachers in self-assessment. See Figure 3.3 for a list of forms that are useful for a mentoring and induction program.

Figure 3.3
Forms for a Mentoring and Induction Program

Form B: *Clinical Observation Notes*—For new teachers to record their observations of experienced teachers

Form C: *Teaching Interview*—For new teachers to use when interviewing experienced teachers

Form D: *Teacher Lesson Reflection*—For the new teacher's self-assessment

Form E: *Informal Classroom Observations*—For the mentor's periodic brief observations of teaching

Form F: *Formal Classroom Observation* and **Form G: *Formal Observation Summary***—For formal observations, including planning and reflection conferences, that may be conducted by the mentor or coach to help prepare the beginning teacher for the more formal evaluation process

Coaching and Professional Development

Most schools and school districts organize their professional development efforts around clearly defined needs developed by the teachers or their supervisors. The framework for teaching can provide the organizing structure for these offerings. Rather than offering training on the latest fad, the school or district can make decisions as to how to invest its limited professional development resources based on evidence.

When teachers conduct a self-assessment of their teaching (using Form I: *Self-Assessment of Practice*), they identify areas of practice they would like to strengthen. Alternatively, when administrators and supervisors conduct formal evaluations of teaching (using Form F: *Formal Classroom Observation* and Form G: *Formal Observation Summary*), they become aware of aspects of teaching (for both individuals and within a school or across an entire district) that could benefit from focused attention.

For example, teachers might determine that they would like to become more proficient in the area of questioning and discussion skills, or in accommodating individual needs in their classrooms. Administrators might find that a number of teachers in a school had identified the same or similar areas for work. Recognizing these patterns can lead naturally to finding a way to meet the identified needs, perhaps through a study group, a workshop, or attendance at a conference.

In addition, educators and professional development specialists have concluded that professional development is most effective when it is embedded into daily practice. That is, when teachers work together, on their own, or with the facilitation of an instructional coach to examine student work and discuss alternate approaches to teaching, they are able to serve as rich resources to one another. See Figure 3.4 for a list of forms that can provide information on which to base ongoing professional development.

Figure 3.4
Forms for Ongoing Professional Development

Form I: *Self-Assessment of Practice*—For teachers to use in analyzing their teaching against accepted standards of practice

＊ ＊ ＊ ＊ ＊

The framework for teaching is a valuable resource for preservice preparation and for ongoing inservice professional development for teachers. It can also provide the structure for the recruitment and hiring of new teachers in a school or a district. The framework provides a common language to inform conversations about practice, enabling those who prepare new teachers and those who support their entry into the profession to make the journey a successful one.

Using the Framework
for Teacher Evaluation

The most frequent use of the framework for teaching is for the evaluation of teacher performance. This is not surprising; school districts are required by law to perform teacher evaluation. Yet many districts' procedures are antiquated and contribute little to the culture of the school. Therefore, when the framework for teaching was first published in 1996, many educators recognized it as an approach to teacher evaluation that had the potential to be much stronger than the procedures they were using at the time.

Both academic and practicing educators agree that among the factors within the school that contribute to student learning, the quality of teaching is the single most important. Thus, of all the important tasks assigned to school leaders, ensuring and promoting high-quality teaching should be paramount; everything else fades in comparison. Nevertheless, many administrators, because of the pressure of immediate demands on their time, don't devote the time or energy to ensuring the quality of teaching that the work deserves.

Because teacher evaluation, particularly for teachers on probation, is a high-stakes matter, it must be conducted responsibly. Evaluators make potentially career-altering decisions about teachers; they should make those decisions based on evidence and ground them in a comprehensive understanding of the criteria of good teaching. It's not acceptable for either teachers or administrators to minimize the process of teacher evaluation; it's too important for that, and, when well done, can contribute much to the culture of professional inquiry in a school.

Of course, it's impossible to either support teaching or evaluate teacher performance without defining the nature of good teaching. Without an agreed-upon description of practice, most evaluators apply their own private, idiosyncratic views of teaching—for example, a preference for a quiet, subdued environment versus a more active one; or for student groups and collaboration versus independent seatwork activities. Many of these preferences are a matter of style, and when applied to evaluation they undermine the fundamental nature of teacher professionalism and judgment. Instead, schools and districts that have adopted the framework for teaching as their definition of good practice are able to locate such preferences within the context of research-based components of teaching, with professional decisions based on their contribution to student learning. Thus, whether students are working in groups or individually is a matter for the teacher to decide, based on the goals for student learning and the characteristics of the group.

Using the framework for teaching as the foundation of a system of teacher evaluation has, in many schools and districts, elevated the requirement for performance appraisal to a professional activity, respectful of teachers' professional judgments. Using the framework contributes to a system that simultaneously ensures quality instruction and promotes professional learning.

Purposes of Teacher Evaluation

Teacher evaluation has two essential purposes: ensuring teacher quality and promoting teacher learning. Although both are critical, they are sometimes seen as being in conflict with one another.

Quality Assurance

As noted, a principal purpose of teacher evaluation is to ensure teacher quality. Schools are, after all, organizations that accept money—from government agencies if they are public schools and directly from parents if they are independent schools. Those investing in schools have a right to expect that their funds will be well used and that the most important aspect of schools—the teaching—is of high quality. This demand is uncompromising, and leaders in every school and school district must be able to assure clients that the quality of teaching is high.

Promoting Professional Learning

In addition to ensuring teacher quality, a system of teacher evaluation seeks to promote professional learning, to aid in the ongoing improvement of teaching. This purpose does not exist because teaching, in general, is of poor quality and must be *fixed*; it exists because teaching is so *difficult* that it is never perfect; no matter how successful a lesson, it could always be improved in some way. In fact, one could argue that part of the professional responsibility of every teacher—like that of members of other professions—is to always seek ways to improve. The teacher evaluation system is another mechanism for contributing to the improvement of teaching.

Reconciling Purposes

Some would argue that these two requirements for a teacher evaluation system—ensuring teacher quality and promoting teacher learning—are fundamentally different from each other and may even be in conflict. That is, a system designed to ensure quality must be rigorous, valid, reliable, defensible (professionally and possibly even legally)—criteria that sound "tough." On the other hand, a system designed to promote learning is likely to be more collaborative, more supportive—"softer," in other words. How can these two demands be reconciled? Some educators have tried to combine them by enhancing the skills of those conducting the evaluations, through such techniques as instructional supervision and cognitive coaching. These techniques are certainly valuable but can only partially address the question of purpose. Instead, resolving what appear to be inconsistent purposes of teacher evaluation involves the *design* of the system itself. The procedures used must respect teacher professionalism and engage teachers in the activities known to promote learning as described in Chapter 2.

The design of teacher evaluation systems is fully described in *Teacher Evaluation to Enhance Professional Practice*, by Charlotte Danielson and Thomas McGreal (ASCD, 2000.) It describes the design elements of a teacher evaluation system that enables evaluators to ensure that teaching is of high quality, using approaches that stimulate teacher self-assessment, reflection on practice, and professional conversation. These strategies yield maximum teacher learning and are reflected in the forms and procedures provided in the book.

A Differentiated Approach

The approach to teacher evaluation supported in this book assumes a differentiated model, in which the needs—of both the teachers themselves and the school districts that employ them—are different for tenured teachers than for nontenured teachers. Nontenured teachers, particularly those new to the profession, need the support of both administrators and mentors in order to consolidate their practice. Furthermore, the tenure decision is a critical one for the district to get right. It is, after all, a lifetime decision; the consequences of a poor decision will be felt for years. The procedures for nontenured teachers are called "Track 1."

On the other hand, tenured teachers are full members of the professional community and should be treated as such. The periodic comprehensive evaluations of tenured teachers should be thorough, and they are likely to be affirming ("Yes, you're still good!"). They can provide an opportunity for high-level professional dialogue between the teacher and the evaluator. During the "other years" of the evaluation process, when a comprehensive evaluation is not occurring, teachers engage in self-directed professional inquiry. The procedures for both phases of the process for tenured teachers are called, collectively, "Track 2."

Lastly, there are occasions (fortunately infrequent) when the performance of a tenured teacher has dropped below standard and must, for the well-being of students, be improved. In those situations, a school district will implement a "Track 3" process, in which teachers are guided in their professional development, under the direction of a supervisor or an evaluator, perhaps with the assistance of an instructional coach.

In summary, then, the evaluation process envisioned in this book is organized as follows:

- Track 1: Novice (or Nontenured) Teachers
- Track 2: Experienced (or Tenured) Teachers—Comprehensive evaluation
- Track 2: Experienced Teachers—Self-directed professional inquiry
- Track 3: Experienced (or Tenured) Teachers—Assistance plan

These approaches and their related issues are described in the sections that follow. Appendix A contains the various forms referred to in the text. See Figure 4.1 for a schedule showing the evaluation activities that teachers and administrators take part in at various times during the year.

Track 1: Novice (or Nontenured) Teachers

With nontenured teachers, it is essential for evaluators to assemble evidence of all aspects of the teacher's performance, including those areas not directly observed in the classroom. On the other hand, it is important to bear in mind that teachers new to the profession may be overwhelmed by the demands of their jobs, so it is unwise to ask them to do more for the evaluation process than is reasonable. Designing the procedures for nontenured teachers involves consideration of a number of questions.

- **Is the evaluation process the same each year, or is it progressive?** Are nontenured teachers evaluated on all the components of the framework for teaching, or does the number increase from one year to the next? Some school districts identify, for example, the 10 most critical components for evaluation the first year, and then add 5 or 6 the second year and an additional 5 or 6 the third year, with all components included by the end of three years.
- **How many formal observations are conducted?** The number of formal classroom observations is usually specified in either statute or negotiated agreements and is typically two to four. Of course, administrators may conduct more than the required number, but typically the minimum is set.

Figure 4.1
Evaluation Schedule

Schedule	Nontenured or Probationary Teacher Activities	Tenured or Continuing Contract Teacher Activities	
		Formal Evaluation Years	Self-Directed Professional Growth Years
Throughout the year	Teacher collects evidence of student learning and professional activities, and administrator conducts informal observations of professional practice.	Teacher collects evidence of student learning and professional activities, and administrator conducts informal observations of professional practice.	Administrator conducts informal observations of professional practice.
August	Administrator informs probationary teachers of the procedures used in the evaluation system.		Teacher conducts self-assessment.
September	Administrator conducts the first formal observation.		Teacher and administrator hold goal-setting conference, unless goals were formulated the previous spring.
October			Teachers form study groups (if possible); formulate growth plans.
November		Administrator conducts first formal observation.	Study groups meet monthly; implement growth plans.
December	Administrator conducts second formal observation.		
January	Administrator and teacher conduct conference about artifacts.	Administrator conducts second formal observation.	
March	Administrator completes annual evaluation; holds conference with teacher.	Administrator and teacher conduct conference about artifacts.	
May		Administrator completes annual evaluation; holds conference with teacher. If appropriate, formulate growth goals for the following year.	Teachers (possibly in groups) and administrator hold reflection conference. If appropriate, formulate growth goals for the following year.

• **Are the observations announced or unannounced?** When an observation is announced, it is possible to conduct a preconference, or planning conference, in which teachers can demonstrate their skills in Domain 1, Planning and Preparation, using the questions in the planning conference protocol. In addition, the teacher can orient the observer to the situation in the class, to prepare the observer for how the lesson is structured and what its principal aims are. On the other hand, an announced observation, precisely because it is announced, may be a "show" lesson, not typical of normal classroom practice.

• **Are extended observations possible?** Most formal observations are confined to the minimum time (for example, 30 minutes) specified in the statute or negotiated agreement. But when an observation is extended (over an entire morning, for example, at the elementary level, or third period over several consecutive days at the secondary level), it is possible to observe aspects of practice that are not revealed in a shorter time. In an elementary classroom, it is possible to see transitions from one activity to another, how the teacher relates one discipline to another, and the handling of routines such as pencil sharpening or restroom breaks. At the secondary level, teachers reveal how concepts are developed over time, how ideas from Thursday, for example, are related to those of Monday. And it's possible to see the variety of approaches a teacher uses. Although extended observations obviously require much more time, they yield information that cannot be obtained in any other way.

• **Which artifacts should be requested?** Nontenured teachers can be asked to provide evidence of their teaching through artifacts. These reveal aspects of teaching not observable in the classroom. Although district evaluation plans should take care not to overwhelm novice teachers with heavy demands, there are some aspects of practice that are critical to know about to make a decision about tenure. These are, typically, evidence of the following:

- Long-range planning (e.g., through a unit plan)
- Student engagement (e.g., through an instructional artifact and student work)
- Communication with families (e.g., through class newsletters or phone logs)
- Professional growth (e.g., through an attendance log of workshops and conferences)
- Participation in a professional community (e.g., through a log of committee service)

Please see Figure 4.2 for a list of forms and instruments that can be used as part of an evaluation system for novice teachers.

Figure 4.2

Forms and Instruments for an Evaluation System for Novice Teachers

Form D: *Teacher Lesson Reflection*—For the new teacher's self-assessment

Form E: *Informal Classroom Observations*—For periodic brief observations of teaching

Form F: *Formal Classroom Observation*—For formal observations, including planning and reflection conferences

Form G: *Formal Observation Summary*—For summarizing a teacher's performance in a formal observation, to be used by an administrator or a supervisor

Artifacts for the nonobserved components (described in Appendix B, Artifacts of Teaching, and summarized on Form H: *Evidence for Domain 4*)

Comprehensive Evaluation

With tenured teachers, the comprehensive evaluation procedures are similar to those for nontenured teachers, and the purpose is essentially the same: for teachers to demonstrate their skill in all the components of the framework for teaching. However, because the teachers are tenured, the assumptions underlying the evaluation procedures are different from those for nontenured teachers. These teachers were awarded tenure status, so the presumption is that they are at least competent. The comprehensive evaluation is, then, an affirmation of the quality of teaching, and it should be designed to enable teachers to demonstrate their skill in all the components of the framework for teaching. Typically a comprehensive evaluation of tenured teachers occurs once every three or four years.

The issues to be considered in designing the details of the system for tenured teachers are, for the most part, the same as those for nontenured teachers, as described earlier. The relevant issues are the following:

- How many formal observations are conducted?
- Are the observations announced or unannounced?
- Are extended observations possible?
- Which artifacts should be requested?

If possible, tenured teachers and their administrators should begin the evaluation cycle with a general discussion about the teacher's overall practice. Questions that could be used (or adapted) for this purpose are those on Form C: *Teaching Interview.* These questions invite teachers to describe the thinking behind various aspects of their teaching, including how they stay abreast of the content they teach, their practices for establishing classroom procedures and standards of student conduct, and their methods for encouraging students to take responsibility for their own learning. In considering how they will respond to such questions, teachers reflect deeply on their practice; when these conversations are part of a comprehensive evaluation system every three or four years, both teachers and administrators can witness the evolution of a teacher's practice over time. Of course, although these conversations may be held with individual teachers, they might also be conducted with teachers in small groups. This practice has the benefit of enabling teachers to hear one another's answers to the questions and to learn from those responses. The practice of all teachers is thereby strengthened.

Because tenured teachers are experienced and take part in a comprehensive evaluation of practice only every three or four years, they can be asked to assemble a portfolio of their practice, demonstrating evidence of all the nonobserved aspects of teaching. A reasonable portfolio could include the following elements:

- A unit plan, including the student assessment plan
- An instructional artifact, with samples of student work, including the teacher's feedback comments to the students
- Examples of record keeping of both instructional and noninstructional material
- Examples of communication with families
- Evidence of contributions to the school and the profession
- Evidence of professional growth
- Evidence of student learning

Appendix B contains guidelines for how to produce documents for a portfolio aligned to the framework for teaching.

The forms and instruments listed in Figure 4.3 can be used as part of an evaluation system for experienced teachers.

Track 2: Experienced Teachers—Self-Directed Professional Inquiry

Self-directed inquiry makes an important contribution to a school's culture of professional inquiry. It is a part of an evaluation system only insofar as it

Figure 4.3
Forms and Instruments for
an Evaluation System for Experienced Teachers

Form C: *Teaching Interview*—For conversations with experienced teachers about their practice.

Form D: *Teacher Lesson Reflection*—For the teacher's self-assessment

Form E: *Informal Classroom Observations*—For periodic brief observations of teaching

Form F: *Formal Classroom Observation*—For formal observations, including planning and reflection conferences.

Form G: *Formal Observation Summary*—For administrator or supervisors to use during a reflection conference, to provide structured feedback on a formal observation.

Artifacts for the nonobserved components (described in Appendix B: Artifacts of Teaching, and summarized on Form H: *Evidence for Domain 4*)

provides the structure for the activities of tenured teachers during the "other" years of the multiyear cycle—that is, the years when a formal evaluation is not conducted. It is not evaluative, in the sense that teachers are not evaluated on the extent to which they achieve their goals. It is pure professional learning. See Chapter 5 for a full description of this phase of the teacher evaluation system.

Track 3: Experienced (or Tenured) Teachers—Assistance Plan

The assistance plan embedded in Track 3 is invoked in the rare circumstances when teachers demonstrate that they are not meeting the district's standards for teaching and formal assistance is required. It is the existence of Track 3—and the willingness of administrators to use it when it is justified—that allows Track 2 to remain a professional approach to teacher evaluation. That is, unless an evaluator is concerned about a teacher's performance, then Track 2, with its two strands of comprehensive evaluation and self-directed professional inquiry, is appropriate. Embedded in Track 2 are two presumptions: competence and continuing learning. The presumption of competence conveys the idea that unless teachers hear something to the contrary, their performance is at least adequate. Although it could always be improved (as could all teaching), the current level of performance is not a cause for concern. But the presumption of continuing learning is needed as well, to convey the notion that regardless of how good a teacher's performance is, the teacher has an obligation to continue to improve. Professional learning never ends; it's a career-long endeavor. Furthermore, for experienced teachers in Track 2, that professional learning is under the teacher's own control through the process of self-directed inquiry.

However, in Track 3 it is the administrator who determines the areas for necessary improvement by the teacher. As part of the formal evaluation procedures used in Track 2 or as a result of informally observed events, the administrator may have concluded that a certain aspect of a teacher's performance must be improved before the teacher can continue in Track 2.

The level of performance that triggers Track 3 must be determined by each school district. Typically, performance at the Unsatisfactory level on any component of the framework for teaching results in an assistance plan to address that issue. Depending on the scale of the problem, the plan might be short term, lasting only a few weeks. Alternatively, a problem identified by an administrator might be less critical in nature but reflect a pattern of low-level (but not unsatisfactory) performance in a number of components. For example, if a teacher who has been teaching for 10 years in the same assignment displays Basic-level performance in a number of components, it could reflect a lack of commitment to improvement. The teacher may have become, in a sense, stuck at the Basic level. In this case, if the district has so decided, the teacher might be placed on an assistance plan to improve in a number of different areas.

As described in *Teacher Evaluation to Enhance Professional Practice* by Danielson and McGreal, some districts identify three phases in Track 3. The first is simply an *awareness phase*, a "heads up," in which a teacher is made aware of a deficiency in performance and an informal plan is developed. For example, the principal may have received phone calls from a number of parents saying that a certain teacher is inaccessible or is not returning messages. Simply mentioning this to the teacher might be enough to motivate a change in approach to family communication; the teacher may be unaware of the parents' impression. If the teacher is involved in a phase of Track 2 (for example, the self-directed professional inquiry), that activity need not be interrupted.

A second phase of Track 3, the *assistance phase*, requires the teacher and the administrator to develop a more formal assistance plan. In this case, the difficulty is seen as more substantive and requiring a formal, written plan. Furthermore, someone other than the principal may be asked to serve as a resource to the teacher. For this more serious deficiency, work on other projects would probably be suspended to enable the teacher to concentrate on addressing the identified problem. An assistance plan typically includes time lines and specific activities for the teacher to undertake, with an established time to check back with the administrator to determine the success of the effort.

The third phase of Track 3 is a *disciplinary phase*, in which lack of success on remedying the difficulty carries real consequences. For example, this phase may take the form of a directive such as this: "The teacher's performance in communicating with families must reach the Proficient level by [date], or the teacher will be referred for dismissal proceedings."

It should be noted that Track 3 is not part of a dismissal process. Although dismissal is not easily accomplished, tenured teachers may be dismissed for incompetence. However, for such action to be defensible, the process used must be transparent; the judgments made must be based on evidence, and teachers must have the opportunity to improve their performance. When these conditions are met, however, as is the case in the procedures in Track 3, then dismissal proceedings (with all their requirements for due process) may begin. But Track 3 is not a prelude to dismissal; rather, it is a good-faith effort by a school district to enable a teacher to strengthen deficient aspects of practice.

Issues in Teacher Evaluation

It's important to consider the issues related to using the framework for teaching for the purpose of teacher evaluation. Fundamentally, evaluative judgments should be based on evidence, and the evidence should be sufficient to support the judgment. A person should be able to discern, from reading the reports of formal and informal observations and the review of artifacts, how an evaluator arrived at a judgment. In other words, an "evidence path" should link the evidence and the judgment. The issues surrounding evaluation are considered here.

The Relationship Between Observation and Evaluation

An observation is not the same thing as an evaluation. An observation provides evidence of the work of teaching; so does a planning conference, or a presentation before a child-study team, or conduct during a faculty meeting. An evaluation, typically done once a year, consists of many different bits of evidence, some of them collected during formal observations of practice, others during informal observations, and others assembled from other aspects of the teacher's work altogether. They are all evidence and are all considered when administrators write an evaluation.

Many administrators, even in districts where a committee has formally adopted the framework for teaching as the foundation for its evaluation system, write their descriptions without referring to the domains and components of the framework. Or, if they do refer to them, they do so in only the most general terms. They supply no actual evidence for a component, rendering their final judgments unsubstantiated.

Using the forms and instruments in this book prompts observers to base their interpretations of classroom events on specific evidence. In completing Form G: *Formal Observation Summary* and Form H: *Evidence for Domain 4*, administrators must indicate the evidence for each of the observed components in the framework for teaching. That is, in using these forms, administrators must be both standards-based and evidence-based in their observations of practice.

The Observation Write-Up

Many administrators spend hours (often on Sunday afternoons at their kitchen tables) producing write-ups of the formal observations they conduct. These typically include a detailed description of the lesson, with judgments about practice. Then, at the bottom of the description, the administrator will indicate the "rating," typically using terms like *unsatisfactory*, *satisfactory*, and *outstanding*. Occasionally the narrative includes some suggestions for improvement, following many complimentary comments about the teacher's skill. It's not clear who the intended audience for these documents is. When asked about that, administrators will say that the intended audience is the teacher. However, experience suggests that when receiving an observation report, most teachers skim it and immediately check the rating. If they like the rating, they might read the report more carefully—but not necessarily; they frequently simply file it. If, of course, they don't like the rating, they may challenge the report. Naturally, many beginning teachers appreciate the validation provided by an administrator's favorable write-up. However, such validation can be supplied through the questions discussed during the reflection conference (the last part of Form F: *Formal Classroom Observation*) and in the summaries of strengths and areas for growth on the final page of Form G: *Formal Observation Summary.*

In fact, the principal audience for an observation write-up is another evaluator who was not present at the lesson. For example, if teachers are observed by more than one administrator within a building, or by both a site administrator and a central office curriculum expert, the second person conducting an observation will want to know what occurred during the first observation and how the events were interpreted by the teacher and the evaluator. Thus the first page of Form G should consist of a brief summary of the lesson—a two- or three-paragraph description of what happened, including *no* judgmental words. (For example, "The students entered the classroom and took their seats calmly. They set to work on a problem on the board while the teacher took roll. The teacher opened the lesson by asking students the following question: . . . .")

Observation write-ups typically raise several issues. Most of these are related to the rating of the individual components of the framework for teaching and to administrative workload.

Rating of individual components. In some schools and school districts, administrators are asked to assign a rating (that is, Unsatisfactory, Basic, Proficient, or Distinguished) for each component of the framework for teaching for each observation. This practice is not recommended, for several reasons.

First, the levels of performance represent levels of performance of *teaching*, not of *teachers*, and performance is notoriously inconsistent, even among highly experienced teachers. Although patterns occur across time and across classes, every day and every hour is different; so performance can vary considerably. Hence, ratings given during an individual class period are just that—a reflection of performance *at that time*. And if one recognizes that the length of time a teacher is observed represents a tiny percentage of the total time the teacher spends with students (perhaps 3 or 4 hours out of 1,000 hours spent with students), one must admit that there is no way to be certain that performance on any given day, at any given hour, is typical of performance in general.

Second, the higher levels of performance (Proficient and Distinguished) reflect, to some extent, experience as well as expertise. Teachers are more likely to demonstrate high levels of performance in May than in September. Furthermore, if a teacher has taught 5th grade for 10 years and is then assigned to a 2nd grade class, the observed performance (at least initially) will not be as high as it would have been in 5th grade.

Third, a teacher's performance is affected to some extent by the characteristics of the students in the class. Although every teacher's goal is to demonstrate Distinguished-level performance every day, in every class, some classes lend themselves more easily or more quickly to becoming the sort of community of learners that undergirds the descriptions of performance at the Distinguished level. For example, members of an AP English class are already committed to the process of school, more so than those enrolled in a basic class, who may be in school reluctantly.

Finally, teachers, like professionals in other fields, want to "look good" and to be regarded as outstanding by their colleagues and superiors. Some are truly perfectionists, who strive for a rating of Distinguished on every component. In other situations, the culture of the school is such that, in the past, every teacher has received the highest rating on whatever scale was being used; therefore, anything less than a Distinguished rating on a component is interpreted as indicating a serious deficiency.

But this practice leads to consequences that undermine the use of the framework for teaching, and the formal observation process, as an opportunity for professional growth:

- When it is important to "look good," many teachers will choose to play it safe, teaching lessons that they know will go smoothly and for which they have prepared their students. They will be unlikely to try a new strategy with the intention of receiving feedback on it from the observer. The "dog and pony show" has been recognized for years as rarely serving a useful purpose but consuming valuable time.

- Teachers will be less willing than they might otherwise have been to take on the difficulty of teaching students known to present challenges. Similarly, they will be less willing to accept a change in assignment.

- If teachers believe they are competing with one another for a limited amount of recognition for excellence, they will be unlikely to share their strategies with one another. The system will undermine other efforts at making practice less private and fostering a spirit of professional inquiry. Some teachers will try to discern, for example, how many Distinguished ratings were earned by their colleagues.

The net result of these varied considerations is that it is unwise for an evaluation system to place high stakes on the outcome of any single observation of teaching. Although the results of every formal observation of teaching contribute to an annual evaluation, many other factors must be considered as well: informal observations of teaching, observations of other aspects of practice (such as participating in a professional community), and the consideration of artifacts that provide evidence of those aspects of teaching that cannot be observed at all.

Administrative workload. Conducting valid and professionally rewarding observations requires time, which is always in short supply. Administrators worry that they simply don't have the time to do what they recognize is the most important aspect of their position—promoting and ensuring good teaching. This situation has no simple remedy, although the forms and procedures in this book can help. That is, if evaluators take notes on the lesson (using Form F: *Formal Classroom Observation*, a similar instrument, or simply a pad of paper), transfer the notes into the relevant components of Form G: *Formal Observation Summary*, and write a brief summary on the first page of Form G, they need not spend much more time writing anything before the reflection conference. The evaluator and the teacher then consider the lesson in light of the levels of performance on Form G and perhaps indicate levels with a highlighter. But the reflection *conversation* is the important part of the process; it yields a summary (written jointly by the teacher and the administrator) of the strengths of the lesson and the areas for growth. Once this conference is completed, the write-up is finished and can be read by other administrators who are also responsible for observing the teacher. The findings can also contribute to the annual evaluation.

Administrators who have compared conducting observations in the traditional manner, with a lengthy narrative write-up, and using the procedures recommended in this book report that the overall time they spend is about the same. But instead of spending most of the time alone, producing the observation report, they spend the time in a meaningful conference with the teacher. They have concluded that time spent in professional conversation is more valuable than time spent in writing.

Chapter 6 contains a description of the specific procedures recommended for this process and a more detailed discussion.

The Evaluation Decision

An annual evaluation represents an evaluator's judgment of a teacher's overall performance over an entire year. And although the person completing the evaluation (generally the principal) may have collected some of the evidence—for example, by conducting a formal observation of teaching—other administrators or supervisors may have been involved as well. The evaluation decision inevitably consists of a number of smaller judgments regarding performance in the classroom, completion of nonclassroom responsibilities (such as communicating with families), and participation in a professional community. In making an evaluation decision, administrators must coordinate information from a number of sources to arrive at a final judgment. And although the levels of performance in the framework for teaching represent a continuum from Unsatisfactory to Distinguished, the evaluation decision is a single judgment: yes or no. Should the probationary teacher be offered a contract for another year or not? Should the 3rd-year teacher be offered tenure or not? These are dichotomous judgments that must somehow be made.

This reality inevitably involves a school district in the matter of setting standards. That is, how good is good enough for a teacher to remain in good standing? How good must performance be for a teacher to "meet or exceed" expectations?" There is no right answer to that question; it is a matter of professional judgment and consensus. Several distinct but related issues are involved in making these decisions; the largest and most controversial has to do with the criteria established for judging teacher performance.

Inputs versus outcomes. The framework for teaching describes the work of teaching; it describes what teachers *do*; that is, it is an input approach. But some argue that it is not sufficient to evaluate teacher performance on the basis of what teachers do. Instead, they maintain, teachers should be evaluated on the basis of the results they achieve with students—on their *outputs*. Hence they have proposed evaluation systems that include, at least for part of the decision, a measure of student learning. The challenges inherent in successfully incorporating information about student learning into an evaluation system have been addressed in Chapter 1.

Weighting. Are all the criteria of good teaching (whether these are the components of the framework for teaching or a combination of judgments about what teachers do and the results they achieve) equally important, or are some more important than others? Are there any components for which deficient performance—regardless of performance in other areas—would indicate inability to perform well overall? Are there any components, in other words, that are deal breakers?

Compensation. This issue has nothing to do with a teacher's pay. Instead it refers to the question of whether excellent performance in some areas can compensate for poor performance in others. Or must a teacher demonstrate performance of a certain level in every component (or domain) of the framework for teaching?

Differentiated expectations. As has been noted many times, teaching is the only profession without a built-in apprenticeship period, such as the internship and residency for physicians. Hence those new to the profession are performing most of their responsibilities for the first time, and their performance is frequently uneven and inconsistent; moments of brilliance alternate with moments when everything is falling apart. This phenomenon is predictable.

As a result, many districts establish the Basic level of performance as their standard for probationary teachers while insisting that most performance be at the Proficient level for teachers to attain tenure. In addition, some school districts become concerned if an experienced teacher, having achieved tenure, demonstrates Basic-level performance in many areas of practice.

However, caution is important in this regard. As noted earlier, performance, although somewhat consistent over time and in different settings, can vary considerably from one day to another. Furthermore, when teachers are assigned to a new grade level or are teaching a course for the first time, they are like new teachers in many important respects; indeed, they *are* new teachers in the new assignment.

Dichotomous judgment versus a multilevel rating. Many schools' and school districts' evaluation systems include a final evaluation in which teachers are awarded a rating, usually Unsatisfactory, Satisfactory, and Outstanding (or Exemplary or some such high rating). Other districts' final evaluation is dichotomous, with teachers either "not meeting" or "meeting or exceeding" expectations or standards. Some districts go so far as to create a formula, or algorithm, for decision making about evaluation levels. The administrators are asked to rate each component and then to use a mathematical process (for example, adding up the scores or averaging them) to arrive at a final rating, with a teacher required to have five, eight, or some other number of components rated at the Distinguished level to achieve a rating of Outstanding.

Although patterns of inadequate performance must be recognized and addressed, those are relatively rare. Rather than rate performance on each component of the framework, it is recommended that school districts rate performance (if at all) at the domain level, based on evidence from many sources (formal and informal classroom observations, other observations of practice, and artifacts) and establish the patterns of performance across all these elements. Then, as long as performance at least meets the district's minimum standards, it does not matter, in terms of consequences, to what extent the performance exceeds those standards. At this stage, the focus of the evaluation process shifts from "rating" to identifying those aspects of practice that could be strengthened; that is, it shifts from summative to formative assessment of teaching. The alternative is not attractive; when schools and school districts rate performance on each component of the framework, then at least some teachers will put energy into challenging the rating, parsing the words, and arguing over evidence.

Some educators argue that a simple dichotomous judgment appears to belittle the work of teaching, that in completing the requirements for a comprehensive evaluation, teachers engage in lots of work. If that work yields only a judgment of "meets or exceeds" expectations, the result feels somewhat disappointing. This is a valid point; teachers, like other professionals, benefit from recognition of their work. But schools and districts should find other ways to recognize excellent teaching—end-of-year celebrations, presentations to colleagues—rather than including recognition of excellence as one of the aims of an evaluation system.

Furthermore, if evaluations take place within a culture of professional inquiry, the stakes are not as high for glowing words and the highest ratings.

That is, if the eventual judgment is only whether a teacher's performance "meets or exceeds" expectations, then the details of the ratings are not so critical.

In some states, the law specifies the form to be used for annual evaluations, and districts are required to use the form unless they obtain a waiver. If this mandated form includes a rating called "Outstanding" or "Exemplary," educators may believe that they have no choice in the matter. However, in most cases the state department of education will willingly grant a waiver if school personnel apply for it and present a good argument for why they want to use a form with only a dichotomous judgment.

Annual evaluation for teachers involved in self-directed professional inquiry. Because a plan for self-directed professional inquiry does not involve formal classroom observations or a predetermined collection of artifacts, some educators find it difficult to envision what form the annual evaluation should take. They conclude—wrongly, it turns out—that because the "normal" evaluation activities do not occur, they cannot make an evaluative judgment at all.

However, although the self-directed inquiry does not involve an evaluation of teaching, it can (and should) involve an evaluation of the performance of the self-directed inquiry itself. It is a process that teachers are expected to take seriously—to select an area for learning on which they can strengthen their practice or a project they want to undertake that can improve the school's offerings for students. Teachers are expected to make a good-faith effort in this project and to have an answer to these questions: "What did you do?" and "What did you learn?" If their answers amount to "Nothing" or if their answers are a waffled version of "Nothing," then they clearly have not made a commitment to the process and would be judged as "not meeting expectations" in the year of self-directed professional inquiry.

✷ ✷ ✷ ✷ ✷

Teacher evaluation is an important use for the framework for teaching. The framework can help establish standards of performance across the full range of teaching responsibilities and enable educators to engage in valuable conversations about practice. Using the framework for teaching in a system of teacher evaluation contributes to a system that is transparent and well understood.

However, it is possible for educators to misuse the framework in an evaluation system, just as any tool may be misused. To reap the full benefit of the framework, it's important for all teachers and administrators to understand the domains and the components and how they are manifested in practice. This is accomplished through training. In addition, the evaluation process must be done in a spirit of respect and professionalism. It can't be, or appear to teachers to be, punitive or contributing to a "gotcha" environment.

5

Using the Framework for Self-Directed Professional Inquiry

One of the most powerful uses of the framework for teaching is as a support for self-directed professional inquiry—the phase of a teacher evaluation system in which experienced teachers take charge of their own professional learning. Self-directed professional inquiry presumes that experienced teachers are skilled in their work and committed to ongoing professional learning. Tenured teachers in good standing typically undertake such work during those years when they are not engaged in a comprehensive evaluation of their practice.

The phase of self-directed inquiry in a teacher evaluation system is not intended to suggest deficiency on the part of teachers. Instead, it is the mechanism through which a school makes explicit its expectations for every teacher to engage in ongoing learning. Although part of the teacher evaluation system, it represents pure professional learning.

Self-directed professional inquiry typically involves several steps. In brief, these are self-assessment, goal setting, action planning, carrying out the plan, reflection and closure, and sharing results with colleagues. (These steps are described in the following sections, and the suggested forms are provided in Appendix A.)

It should be noted that teachers should not be judged on the extent to which they achieve their goals. A moment's reflection will demonstrate why this is so. If teachers are to be judged on the extent to which they achieve their goals, they are likely to select goals they know they can achieve. That is, the goals that at least some teachers set will be low-level goals; other teachers may choose to work in an area in which they are already proficient.

The overall aim of the self-directed inquiry is for teachers to engage in new learning, to take on an area that may require them to stretch. The procedures should not make that less likely. However, if a teacher disregards the process of self-directed professional inquiry or doesn't take the process seriously, such behavior *is* a performance issue and would have to be addressed by an administrator.

Self-Assessment

Any project or self-directed study a teacher undertakes must be grounded in self-assessment; it must reflect a need the teacher feels for improvement of teaching. The study can reflect any aspect of practice, and the self-assessment can take several different approaches, including the following:

• Using Form I: *Self-Assessment of Practice*, teachers can consider their own practice against the levels of performance in the framework for teaching. By circling or highlighting the statements that best reflect one's performance, it is not difficult to determine areas of relative weakness, those aspects of teaching that could benefit from focused attention.

• Teachers can assess the evolution of content in the subjects they teach and determine that they need to bolster their mastery of that content.

• Teachers can survey recent developments in pedagogical research and determine whether there is one that they have not yet investigated sufficiently to incorporate into their everyday practice. Examples might be an approach such as cooperative learning or the use of primary-source documents in teaching history.

• The school or district might have recently adopted an instructional approach unfamiliar to many teachers. For example, an inquiry science program or a new approach to literacy might present challenges that require teachers to acquire new skills. Similarly, school or district initiatives or goals (such as writing across the curriculum) might have implications for teachers as they embark on self-directed inquiry.

• The school or district might be undergoing significant demographic changes, requiring all teachers to learn about different world cultures. For example, a significant number of Cambodian families might have moved into the area recently, and teachers may need to learn about the ethnic group's backgrounds and traditions to help those students be successful in school.

Goal Setting

A critical step in the self-directed professional inquiry is the establishment of goals for professional growth. It is essential to recognize that these goals are goals for the *teacher's* learning, not student learning. A teacher's goal for learning may well have been suggested by a need to strengthen skill in an area of practice that is revealed in weak student performance, but the goal itself is about the teacher's learning. For example, a school might have a goal to improve student performance in mathematics problem-solving skills. The teacher's goal with respect to this initiative, however, is not to improve student mathematics problem solving. Rather, it may be to learn new instructional strategies to support student learning in that area.

This doesn't mean that a teacher's goal should be unrelated to student learning. We know that student learning is the consequence of everything that occurs in school. Indeed, low student achievement in some area might lead a teacher to decide to focus on a particular goal. But general instructional skills, such as learning how to structure cooperative learning activities, is unlikely to result in improved student achievement in the short term. Therefore, the teacher's goal should be stated in terms of the teacher's own learning.

Other questions to consider in goal setting include the following:

- How many goals should a teacher set?
- What is the relationship between a teacher's goals for professional growth and school and district goals?
- What are the characteristics of good professional growth goals?

The following sections address these questions.

Number of Goals

Typically, teachers set one to three goals. If a goal represents a significant amount of learning, one goal may be sufficient. If each goal involves small amounts of learning, it's not unrealistic to undertake two or three.

Individual Goals Versus School and District Goals

Goals established by schools and districts may be appropriate for inclusion in a teacher's individual goals for professional growth; it depends on the situation. Some district goals relate to aspects of the district operation to which teachers don't directly contribute, such as completing a building project. But for those goals that address student learning, it is important for teachers to translate those goals into their own efforts, where appropriate.

For example, a high school seeking improvement in students' writing skills might ask all teachers, in all subjects, to incorporate student writing into their courses. A science teacher could well incorporate learning how to teach students to write about science into a professional growth goal. However, a math teacher might have concentrated on this area several years ago, so a focus on student writing in mathematics would not represent new learning for that teacher.

Alternatively, a physical education teacher might well have limited opportunities to ask students to write and so might decide not to incorporate the district goal into a set of individual goals. Simply stated, whether teachers' professional growth goals reflect district or building goals depends on whether they are suitable to the individuals concerned.

Characteristics of Good Goals for Professional Growth

Not all goals represent valuable pursuits for a teacher's professional learning. In general, viable goals share certain characteristics. Figure 5.1 provides examples of worthwhile and defective goals.

• The goal should be related to the teacher's responsibilities. This requirement would disqualify a goal such as pursuing an administrative credential or learning a skill (that one does not teach) purely for personal reasons, such as pottery or ballroom dancing.

• The goal should not be part of a teacher's everyday teaching responsibilities. Thus, for example, "implementing the new reading program" is not a growth goal; it is part of the teacher's job responsibilities. However, it is possible that implementing a new program—for example, in science—will require a teacher to learn important new skills, such as how to guide students in scientific inquiry. The learning of those skills would represent valuable new learning.

• The goal should be something important to the teacher. This is not to deny an important role for an administrator in helping a teacher clarify an approach or locate resources. But if the administrator is dictating the goal, then it is no longer the teacher's goal. Of course, if during the year of a comprehensive evaluation certain areas of teaching were identified as relatively weak, it would be sensible for a teacher to choose to strengthen those areas. But the choice should be the teacher's. If an administrator believes it essential for a teacher to improve in some aspect of teaching, then the administrator should invoke Track 3, in which the teacher is put on an improvement plan. Otherwise, it is the teacher's choice.

• A goal may be stated in terms of a project or action research. To investigate the effectiveness of a certain practice or to create some new materials to help students understand the European settlers' expansion into the western territories from the natives' point of view would certainly qualify as viable goals.

• Goals should be stated as outcomes, not as activities. Therefore, taking students on a study trip to the aquarium is not a professional growth goal. However, developing a curriculum incorporating the resources of the aquarium could be.

• As part of establishing a goal, a teacher should be able to indicate what would count as evidence of success. This indication should be stated in specific terms rather than a general statement such as "Students will improve their reading

Figure 5.1
Goal Analysis

Statement	Goal?	Comment
I'm in a master's program and need to finish my dissertation this year. That's my primary goal for the year.	No	Goals should relate to the teacher's learning about a new skill or technique or about student learning. This goal is an appropriate goal for a teacher's professional advancement but not for a focus during a year of professional inquiry.
I want to implement the new reading series.	No	Every teacher in the school is obliged to implement the new reading series. This is a requirement of employment. However, if the new reading series includes an approach to teaching literature that is unfamiliar, the goal might be written like this: "I want to improve my teaching of literature so the students both enjoy it and become proficient at literary analysis."
I'm working with a new team this year. My goal is to concentrate on teaming.	Maybe	This statement is not clear as to what is meant by "concentrate on," and it's possible that in practice this goal would result simply in a teacher's attending team meetings as scheduled. A better way to state this goal could be this: "I am working with a new team this year, and I will be facilitating some of the meetings. I want to learn how to help a group function productively."
I want to create rubrics to use in my classes, especially for long-term projects.	Yes	Although this goal is not stated in terms of teacher learning, creating rubrics inevitably involves considerable learning. The action plan would, presumably, spell out an iterative process of developing rubrics, trying them with student projects, and then revising them based on the experience. That process reflects real learning.
I need to find a more effective way to cover the material in my history classes so students can go into greater depth.	Yes	This goal would be better stated like this: "I want to learn how to teach my history classes in such a way that students go into greater depth but also learn all the important material." This involves understanding student learning and motivation, trying new techniques, and evaluating their results.
I'm teaching 3rd grade for the first time. My goal is to become familiar with the 3rd grade curriculum.	No	Becoming familiar with the 3rd grade curriculum is essential to being successful in that assignment. But gaining such familiarity involves work that is critical to the teacher's position and does not represent new learning for the teacher.
I'm new to the system so I want to be sure I know the discipline policies and follow them in my classroom.	No	This goal represents the work all teachers new to a school must undertake, and it illustrates the steep learning curve that is inherent in any new assignment. But it is, essentially, a matter of implementing school policies, not engaging in new learning related to instruction.
I want to get parents more involved in their children's education.	Maybe	Whether this is a goal or not depends on the reason behind the statement. If the teacher intends to simply reach out to parents, it simply represents work teachers must do as part of their assignment. However, if the teacher has been trying to engage parents but has not succeeded, the goal might represent the teacher's desire to learn new techniques to reach parents of a different culture or parents who are recent immigrants to the area. This new learning would, therefore, be the goal, with increased parent involvement as evidence that the teacher had been successful.

skills." Stating evidence may require the teacher to collect data of some sort, as appropriate to the goal. If the goal is a project to ascertain the effectiveness of a new instructional strategy, samples of student work would be appropriate. If the goal relates to a teacher's use of a general approach, such as differentiation of instruction, the evidence would consist of the teacher's documentation of how she differentiated, and the results achieved.

Action Planning

A professional growth plan is a document that outlines the activities teachers will undertake in pursuing their goals for professional growth. These plans need not be elaborate; in fact, the simpler they are the better. The plan should include a reasonable sequence of activities the teacher expects to do in pursuing the goal and estimated completion dates for each activity. The plan can include various types of activities, such as reading books or articles, taking a workshop or course, conferring with colleagues, observing colleagues who are skilled in the area one is pursuing, trying new strategies in one's own class, or inviting a colleague or administrator to observe and provide feedback.

The plan should also include needed resources, if any. For example, if a teacher wants to observe colleagues or to invite a colleague to observe and provide feedback, class coverage may be needed. Or if a teacher intends to read books or articles that are not in the school's professional library, they could be acquired and then made available to other faculty.

Other teachers in the school may be working on a similar topic, in which case they can work together in a study group. The administrator may be the individual who is most aware of the interests of different members of the faculty and can facilitate the formation of such groups.

Form J: *Individual Professional Development Plan* provides a structure for goal setting and action planning. A sample plan is provided as Figure 5.2.

Carrying Out the Plan

For serious professional learning to occur, teachers must devote time to the effort. And if several teachers have identified similar goals to pursue, they can frequently achieve more if they work together. But actually doing the activities one has identified in a plan is sometimes a challenge. Teaching is, after all, demanding work. But if ongoing professional learning is recognized as important to effective performance, teachers must take it seriously.

Some schools and districts carve out protected time for teachers to pursue their professional growth plans. For example, if one day a week after school is reserved for faculty meetings, some schools decide that one of those meetings

Figure 5.2
Individual Professional Development Plan

Teacher _____   School _____

Grade Level(s) _____ Subject(s) _____   Date _____

Based on your self-assessment, your administrator's input, and any school or district initiatives, what goal have you identified? What is an area of knowledge or skill that you would like to strengthen?
I intend to enhance my skills in cooperative learning, and the use of group work in my teaching.

Describe the connection between this goal and your teaching assignment.
I teach middle school social studies; many of the topics lend themselves to group work, but I don't have the confidence in my skill to incorporate them in the classroom.

What would success on this goal look like? How will you know when you have achieved it? What would count as evidence of success?
1. *Students will be able to assume different roles in group work.*
2. *An observer would notice students working productively together, with all students contributing.*
3. *Students themselves will report that they find group strategies productive for learning.*

Describe the activities you will do to work toward your goal, and appropriate time lines.

Activity	Time Line
	These activities will be completed by
I plan to	
1. Read two articles and a book on cooperative learning.	September 30
2. Enroll in a weekend course devoted to cooperative learning.	October 31
3. Observe two teachers in the school who use cooperative learning and discuss their techniques with them.	November 30
4. Teach my students the skills of respectful group work, and about the different roles in group work.	December 15
5. Begin incorporating group work into my classes, where appropriate.	February 15
6. Invite a colleague to observe my class while students are engaged in group work to offer me feedback.	March 31
7. Make a faculty presentation to share what I have learned.	May 30

What resources will you need to better achieve your goal?
- *Books and journals from the school's professional library.*
- *Tuition for the weekend course.*
- *Class coverage to enable me to visit colleagues' classrooms, if it's not possible during my preparation time.*

each month will be covered through written material and the time will be made available for teachers to work on their plans. Other schools designate one morning a week before school as a protected time for professional learning. If teachers are working together, joint time is critical, and this kind of scheduling can provide it.

Most states now require teachers to renew their license to teach every five years or so; that is, instead of a life-time certificate, states grant a five-year (or some other number) renewable license. The typical process for renewal is through demonstrated participation in a certain number of hours of professional development activities. Many schools and districts have aligned their requirements for self-directed inquiry to their state's requirements for license renewal so the same activities satisfy both.

In some schools, educators have found it advisable to schedule a mid-year check-in meeting with the administrator to discuss how things are going, whether unexpected obstacles have surfaced, and any other relevant matters. Such a meeting can also help ensure that the work on the plan is actually proceeding and that it has not fallen to the bottom of the teacher's to-do list. Teachers can use Form K: *Individual Professional Development Log of Activities* to keep track of what they have done with respect to their plan.

Reflection and Closure

The last—and critical—step in self-directed professional inquiry is reflection and closure. As with reflection on classroom practice, the reflection step is, arguably, the most important of the entire process.

An established protocol is recommended for this reflection; a protocol ensures both consistency from one teacher (or one school) to another and that teachers are able to prepare adequately for the reflection conference. Again, the purpose of a reflection conference is not to "trick" teachers or to convey a "gotcha" message. Rather, it is to enable teachers to engage in systematic reflection on what has been, it is hoped, a valuable process of professional learning. Form L: *Reflection on the Individual Professional Development Plan (IPDP)* may be used for this purpose.

Teachers and administrators should plan to devote at least 30 minutes to the reflection conference. However, it is possible for several teachers to meet jointly with an administrator for this purpose; in that case, it would require more than 30 minutes total, but not as long as if each conference were conducted individually. Such a procedure has the enormous benefit of enabling teachers to learn from one another's projects.

Moreover, if a district has adopted a three- or a four-year evaluation cycle, the reflection and closure conference at the end of one year can serve as the goal-setting conference for the following year. That is, rather than a September-through-May schedule, teachers can work on a May-through-May schedule. Such a revision makes the entire process far more efficient and permits teachers to enroll in a summer course that contributes to the professional development identified in their plan.

Sharing Results with Colleagues

Although not a formal part of the process of self-directed professional inquiry, a final step of sharing results with colleagues is highly recommended. This activity is particularly powerful if teachers have worked in teams or study groups to engage in a professional inquiry. This step merits consideration for two primary reasons.

First, setting aside prime time for collegial sharing reinforces the concept that every school has professional educators who know a lot about their practice and from whom other educators can learn. That is, it is not necessary to attend outside conferences or workshops to enhance one's professional skill; the resources needed for much professional learning are available in every school. Furthermore, professional sharing enhances the concept of a culture of professional inquiry—an important part of a school's overall culture.

Second, when teachers know that they will be asked to describe their professional activities for their colleagues and inform others about what they have learned during their self-directed inquiry, they devote greater energy to it. In some schools where teachers are asked to develop goals for professional growth each year, many teachers don't take it seriously; with respect to the form they must complete, they ask, "What shall I write down this year?" If an individual professional growth plan does not seriously address genuine professional issues being dealt with by teachers, it can easily revert to a meaningless exercise in compliance. If, however, teachers know that they will be asked at the end of the year to tell their colleagues what they have worked on and what they have learned from the experience, they tend to take it seriously. Many teachers would have taken it seriously without that external impetus, but for some the prospect of sharing can make a significant difference.

Schools and school districts create different procedures for this sharing of results. Some invite teachers to share what they have been doing and learning at regularly scheduled faculty meetings within the school. Others designate a professional development day in which teachers from different schools come together and hear from their colleagues according to a prepared schedule. The resulting sharing is a powerful reminder that teachers in different schools serve the same group of students and that they can all strengthen their practice if they learn from one another.

✳ ✳ ✳ ✳ ✳

Self-directed professional inquiry is a powerful way that the framework for teaching can support teacher learning and development. Teachers can use the framework to conduct an assessment of their practice and to create an action plan based on that assessment. Such inquiry supports the concept that teaching is an important profession that educators continue to learn about throughout their careers.

Recommended Procedures for Teacher Evaluation

The experience of hundreds of educators has provided important insights into the many procedural matters related to the various aspects of teacher evaluation—conducting formal and informal observations, assembling and reviewing evidence of the components in Domain 4 of the framework for teaching, and completing the annual evaluation. This chapter covers these recommended procedures in depth. The lists of procedures in each section are a summary of steps, written from the observer's point of view, and they represent an amalgam of practices that educators have found to be effective. Modify them to suit your situation. See Appendix A for the forms mentioned in this chapter.

Formal Classroom Observation

A formal observation typically consists of observing an entire lesson, lasting at least 30 minutes. The minimum time for the observation is usually spelled out in a district's negotiated agreement. The process often includes a preconference, or planning conference; the observation itself; and a postconference, or reflection conference. A formal observation is usually conducted as part of teacher evaluation, but mentors may conduct one to help a new teacher be more successful in the formal evaluation conducted by a supervisor.

Purpose

The purpose of a formal classroom observation is to directly acquire evidence of teachers' practice in their interactive work with students. The observation is "formal" in the sense that the observer remains in the class for at least the amount of time specified in the negotiated agreement and the observation results in a written document. The observation may be either announced or unannounced; if announced, it should begin with a planning conference, during which the teacher describes the plan for the lesson.

The formal classroom observation is central to any approach to mentoring, coaching, or teacher evaluation because a teacher's interaction in the classroom with students is rightly regarded as central to the work of teaching. It does not constitute the whole of teaching, to be sure, but excellent teaching always includes superior classroom performance.

In many schools and districts, the formal classroom observation is the centerpiece of the evaluation process; indeed, in some places the term *evaluation* is used to refer to the observation. Of course, as important as it is, classroom observation is merely the source of evidence of practice. Hence, although it plays a central role in any system of teacher evaluation, what is observed should not be thought of as constituting the whole of teaching.

Discussion

As noted earlier, the formal classroom observation consists of three distinct elements: a preconference, or planning conference; the observation itself; and a postconference, or reflection conference. If the observation is unannounced, a planning conference is not possible; but many of the questions from the planning conference protocol may be adapted and used during the reflection conference.

Form F: *Formal Classroom Observation* provides protocols for use in both the planning and reflection conferences. The questions should be modified, as needed, to suit particular situations. Teachers should know the questions in advance; the purpose of the observation is not to try to "trick" teachers, but rather to offer them the opportunity to display their planning skills. Some teachers may want to prepare for the conferences by making notes in response to the questions; others will prefer simply to think about the questions and be prepared to discuss them. That decision should be left up to the teachers. The key point is that they know in advance what they will be asked to discuss.

It is not recommended that teachers be asked to write full answers to the questions in the planning and reflection conferences. Written responses not only add to the teacher's burden; they also make it more likely that the administrator will ask that the responses be left in the office and will skip the conference. But the most important aspect of both conferences (especially the reflection conference) is the conversation that takes place.

As part of the planning conference, the teacher should bring a copy of any written material (such as worksheets or directions for an activity) the students will be using during the lesson. Consideration of this material, its design and its level of cognitive challenge, provides a window into a critical aspect of the teacher's planning skills. Many teachers are highly capable at interaction with students but have not yet acquired the skill of designing, or selecting and adapting, good work for students. That is, they may use a worksheet provided in their instructional materials uncritically, or assign a page in the textbook when, if they were to give it a little thought, they could develop an activity that would be far more effective in engaging students in significant learning.

Then, during the reflection conference, examination of some samples of student work from the assignment (representing a range of abilities in the class) provides direct evidence of the extent of student engagement and the degree of understanding. Of course, not all situations will lend themselves to the collection of student work, but when available, student work can provide a valuable insight into classroom practice and student engagement.

If the school or district has an established lesson planning form, teachers could be asked to complete it before a formal classroom observation. Such a form is not included in the materials in this book because it is not considered essential to the process. However, some schools require such an exercise, and in some places the requirement is formalized in the negotiated agreement. In those cases, the lesson planning form, rather than the questions in the planning conference protocol, could be used to structure the planning conference.

For some purposes, particularly mentoring and coaching, it is customary to ask teachers what they would particularly like the observer to focus on during the lesson. For example, a teacher might be working on improving questioning skills or on making smoother transitions between activities. In that case, the teacher might want specific feedback from the observer on those matters. However, when a formal observation is conducted to contribute to an evaluation, it is important that the observer collect evidence of all the components of the framework that are demonstrated.

Observers should take notes during the observations, either on blank sheets of paper or on Form F: *Formal Classroom Observation*. If using the form, observers are prompted to note the time of events they record. Later they can return to their notes and assign them to components of the framework for teaching.

Many administrators have been trained to make a complete script of the lesson, writing as much as they can about what they observe. Depending on the complexity of the situation, this may be difficult to do and may result in, at best, a record of what is said, typically by the teacher. And if the teacher speaks a lot, writing down everything said may result in the observer being unable to look around during virtually the entire lesson, missing much of what the students do, how the room is arranged, and other matters. It is essential that an observer's notes consist of evidence only, not the observer's interpretation or opinion about what occurred during the lesson. The notes that are completed during the lesson should be free of adjectives or adverbs that suggest how well something was done; they should contain only facts.

Of course, taking notes during an observation involves making choices in deciding what to write and what to ignore. Classrooms are complicated places; there is, typically, a lot going on. Therefore, observers' notes should be recorded with the future use of those notes in mind. An observer who will be evaluating a nontenured teacher, for example, must ultimately be able to supply evidence of the teacher's performance on all the components of the framework for teaching. Any single lesson, of course, may not include evidence of all of the components; but over time the teacher should demonstrate all of them—and at a satisfactory level of performance. Therefore, observers must know the framework sufficiently well to recognize when they have neglected to record information from a certain area of teaching that, while present, they may have simply ignored.

Classroom notes should include not only what the teacher says and does, but also questions, statements, and actions by students. And nonverbal as well as verbal communication is important. Some observers make a point of capturing as much as possible of the students' experience during the lesson, recording student interactions with one another, expressions of confusion, and the like. And, of course, the appearance of the classroom, the manner in which the teacher has modified the physical environment to support the lesson, is also important information for an observer to record.

If possible, the observer should provide the teacher with a copy of the observation notes shortly after the lesson. This gesture is for purposes of accuracy only: did the observer see the important elements of the lesson? Some observers choose not to do this, primarily because the notes, if handwritten, are difficult to read. Other observers find that they make notes to themselves in the margins that they would prefer not to share with the teacher—at least not yet. Whether the notes are provided to the teacher before the reflection conference is a matter for individuals to decide; the principal advantage is that providing the notes conveys transparency in the entire system.

It is important that observers, whether they are mentors, coaches, or evaluators, not consider a teacher's level of performance on any of the components of the framework for teaching while observing in the classroom. Making such a judgment would be premature. The purpose of the observation is simply to collect evidence; the interpretation of that evidence against the levels of performance comes after the observer leaves the classroom and has an opportunity to consider all the bits of evidence pertaining to a certain component.

Therefore, following the observation and before the reflection conference, the observer should do two things. First, the observer should write a brief summary (a few paragraphs only), recording the major events of the lesson on the first page of Form G: *Formal Observation Summary*. This summary should contain sufficient detail so that if it were read by someone who was not present, the principal structure of the lesson would be clear. Second, the observer should consider the observation notes in light of the framework for teaching and write examples of evidence observed in the space following each component on Form G. Then the observer should consider all the evidence for a given component as a whole and indicate on the form (for example, by using a highlighter) the sentences or phrases in the descriptions of the levels of performance that best characterize the lesson. The observer will take the *Formal Observation Summary* to the reflection conference and use it during the conversation with the teacher.

The value of observations for teachers is greatly enhanced if they have the opportunity for systematic self-assessment and reflection on the lesson before the reflection conference. After all, more important than a flawless lesson is the teacher's awareness of when events became derailed and understanding of how to correct the problem. Furthermore, the questions in the reflection conference protocol (provided as the last page of Form F: *Formal Classroom Observation* and the first page of Form D: *Teacher Lesson Reflection*) are designed to engage the teacher in reflection on all the important decisions that were made in the design of the lesson: the selection of learning outcomes, the design of activities, grouping of students, choice of materials, and so on. It is almost never the case that a lesson was "great" or "terrible." More likely, certain aspects of the lesson were successful; others less so. The important thing is for teachers to know which were which. Therefore, by engaging in a conversation during the postconference, teachers (particularly novice teachers) begin to acquire important skills of in-depth reflection; the goal is for these to become habits of mind for a teacher following any lesson.

If both the teacher and the observer have analyzed the lesson in light of the framework for teaching before the reflection conference, then that meeting, in addition to the discussion stimulated by the questions on the conference protocol, consists of comparing notes. Often they will have identified the same areas of success and areas that need attention. Sometimes they may disagree, in which case they should determine the source of disagreement.

If areas of disagreement exist and if the observation is part of an evaluation, it is, of course, the administrator's view that counts in the end. However, disagreements are rare, and for most educators the opportunity to engage in a professional conversation about a lesson constitutes the most valuable aspect of the entire process.

As part of the reflection conference and as a result of the conversation about the lesson, the teacher and the observer complete the last page of the *Formal Observation Summary* together, noting the areas of strength and any areas for growth. Completing this section of the document together offers certain advantages. First, when completed jointly, the written summary reflects the views of both parties. Second, when the document is completed during the reflection conference, the paperwork for the observation is complete, and the mentor, coach, or administrator does not have to spend time after the observation preparing a write-up. The observation summary, to which both have contributed and which both have signed to indicate that they have conducted a conversation about the lesson, *is* the write-up. The brief summary on page 1 of the *Formal Observation Summary*, the evidence and interpretations of that evidence for each of the components in Domains 1, 2, and 3 of the framework observed during the lesson, and the description of strengths and areas for growth are sufficient to contribute to an annual evaluation. They can also convey enough information to another evaluator (in situations where teachers are observed by more than one individual) to enable that person to continue supporting the teacher.

Procedures

1. Conduct a preconference (planning conference) using the questions in the Interview Protocol for a Planning Conference (page 1 of Form F: *Formal Classroom Observation*) and taking notes on the teacher's response to each question. As part of the planning conference, if appropriate, discuss written materials (worksheets, directions) that students will be using during the lesson.

Note: Teachers should have a copy of the questions before the conference and be prepared to discuss them. If they so choose, teachers could make notes before the conference, but this is not necessary.

2. Ask the teacher to collect, if appropriate, several samples of student work from the lesson, representing a range of abilities in the class, to be discussed at the postconference (reflection conference).

3. Observe the lesson, taking notes on the appearance of the classroom and the actions and statements by teachers and students. Write these notes on pages 2 and 3 (add more if needed) of Form F. Make every effort to write only *evidence*, not your *opinion* or *interpretation* of what you see and hear. Leave the right-hand column blank; after the observation, you will write the components represented by each line of your notes.

4. (Optional) Give a copy of your notes to the teacher for review before the postconference.

5. Complete the right-hand column of Form F, indicating the components represented by each item in your notes.

6. On Form G: *Formal Observation Summary*, write a brief summary of the lesson, including what the teacher was hoping to achieve, the major activities, and other pertinent matters. Then, for Domains 1, 2, and 3, consider each component of the framework for teaching and indicate a few pieces of evidence from the lesson for each one, as appropriate. If you have no evidence for a

component, leave it blank. Then, using a highlighter, indicate the sentences or phrases in the level of performance that best captures the evidence cited.

7. Ask the teacher to reflect on the lesson, considering the questions on the first page of Form D: *Teacher Lesson Reflection.* Also ask the teacher to complete a self-assessment of the lesson, indicating on the following pages of the form her perceived level of performance for each component, citing specific evidence for the choice.

8. Conduct the postconference (reflection conference), using the questions on the last page of Form F: *Formal Classroom Observation* and on the first page of Form D: *Teacher Lesson Reflection* (the questions are the same, with the exception of Form D's Question 7, which asks the teacher to consider the lesson in light of the components of the framework for teaching.) Discuss the levels of performance for each component assigned by both you and the teacher, discussing in particular those about which you disagree.

(Optional) Determine, together if possible, the level of performance for each domain. On Form G, indicate the level of performance for each domain by checking an option in the Rating section: U for Unsatisfactory, B for Basic, P for Proficient, and D for Distinguished. Provide feedback on the lesson, as appropriate.

9. Write a brief summary (with the teacher's participation, if possible) of the principal strengths and areas for future learning revealed in the lesson. If time permits, this should be accomplished during the reflection conference itself. Write these comments on the last page of Form G.

10. Sign the document, indicating that the conversation regarding the lesson has been conducted.

11. If you have decided to assign a rating for each domain, transfer these ratings to Form M: *Summary of Observations and Artifacts.*

Informal Classroom Observations

Informal classroom observations of teaching take place unannounced; they may last only 5 or 10 minutes. They do not result in any formal write-up, and whether the information gathered can be used as evidence in a teacher's evaluation is typically a matter that is specified in the district's negotiated agreement.

These observations constitute an important manifestation of an administrator or a supervisor serving as a school's instructional leader. By spending time informally in classrooms and conducting conversations with the teachers later about what was observed, supervisors can help shape teachers' thinking and instruction.

Informal classroom observations are also important to mentors and coaches. By stopping in to visit classrooms, they can see what a teacher is doing and gain an informal sense of potential areas for further learning for the teacher. Because mentors and coaches have no evaluative authority over teachers, they can walk into a classroom without having an impact on the teacher; things can continue in a completely natural manner. This informality permits later discussions to be relaxed, without a teacher feeling threatened by the situation.

Purpose

The purpose of informal classroom observations is to enable principals and supervisors to keep their finger on the pulse of the school and to serve as an informal resource to teachers as they strive to improve their practice. In addition, as part of a system of teacher evaluation, informal classroom observations provide an ongoing source of evidence of a teacher's practice in a natural setting; this evidence can contribute to an annual evaluation and may provide a more accurate window on an individual's teaching than the evidence that is derived through more formal observations.

Discussion

It is possible to observe much about classroom practice during even a short visit. For example, the general tone of the class will be evident, as will other aspects of Domain 2 (The Classroom Environment). The observer may or may not see enough of a lesson to be able to conclude much about Domain 3 (Instruction), because there may not be the opportunity to observe, for example, how the teacher develops an idea. However, the observer may see the extent to which students are engaged in learning, the quality of questions posed by both students and teacher, and the use of assessment in instruction. In addition, an observer may see evidence (although probably limited) of Domain 1 (Planning and Preparation)—for example, the teacher's knowledge of the content and familiarity with the students.

It is not necessary to take detailed or extensive notes during an informal classroom observation. Indeed, during a brief classroom visit there is not time to do so. But the notes should be sufficient to add bits of evidence onto Form E: *Informal Classroom Observations*. If an observer, for example, notices a teacher offering encouragement to a student or making a specific effort to include all students in a discussion, such actions are worth noting.

Notes from an informal classroom observation will probably be written simply on a blank pad of paper. Then, before the memory has faded, the observer should quickly fill in the relevant sections of Form E, noting the date of the observation and the concept being taught. Then, from the notes, the observer can fill in evidence as appropriate to the different components of the framework for teaching.

A question to consider concerns whether observers dropping in for a brief visit should meet with the teacher after the observation, or leave a note, or do nothing. They should at least be consistent about what sort of feedback or comments they offer to teachers following an informal, brief visit. Otherwise teachers will interpret silence or a note as evidence of deficiency. Novice teachers will appreciate a note or a few words of encouragement. More experienced teachers also value such comments. But an observer can do more; it's possible to engage in a more in-depth conversation about the lesson, inquiring about what occurred the previous day and whether the behavior of certain students was typical. These conversations can be very rich and may be conducted informally, during a lunch break or in the principal's office later in the day.

Of course, if an administrator observes events in a classroom during an informal classroom observation that indicate performance at an Unsatisfactory level on the levels of performance—that is, if harm is being done to students—it is imperative that the administrator schedule a conference with the teacher for later in the day. Fortunately such episodes are rare. Much more typically the observer will see events in the classroom that inspire interest in learning more.

Many administrators find that, in spite of their best intentions, it is difficult to find the time for informal observations of teaching. This is regrettable, because it is an important activity, providing the most accurate information possible about classroom teaching. Administrators who are successful in this effort are those who exercise great discipline and make a commitment to spend, for example, one morning each week visiting classrooms. Touching base with every teacher every few weeks is an important way to stay connected with what different teachers are doing and what issues they are addressing in their teaching. By conducting informal observations and engaging in professional conversations about practice, administrators are able to serve as resources to the teachers in their schools.

Procedures

1. Observe a class briefly, but for at least five minutes.

2. Take notes on different aspects of the lesson, as appropriate.

3. If desired, leave a note for the teacher with a brief supportive comment about some aspect of the lesson.

4. Arrange to speak with the teacher, even briefly, about any aspect of what you observed that warrants such a conversation. This should be considered a professional conversation, in which you are able to serve as a resource to the teacher in thinking through the events of the lesson.

5. Complete the first page of Form E: *Informal Classroom Observations*, noting the date of the observation and the concept being taught. Then transfer your notes to the relevant section for the different components of the framework for

teaching, making comments as appropriate. Do not indicate any levels of performance; this will be done following multiple informal observations.

6. At the end of the year, complete the pages on Form E, indicating the levels of performance reflected by the collective evidence from the informal observations. Transfer these notations to Form M: *Summary of Observations and Artifacts*.

Other Observations of Practice

Teachers demonstrate their skill in many ways and in many settings. They interact with students in the hallways, in lunchrooms, and on playgrounds; they participate in faculty meetings; they meet with parents and conduct parent presentations. In short, teaching involves far more than what many noneducators think of as teaching—namely, working with students in the classroom.

Purpose

The purpose of conducting other observations of practice is for administrators to evaluate performance and for administrators, mentors, and coaches to support teachers in their development of skill in all the myriad aspects of teaching that go beyond the classroom walls. Such observations are an important component of evaluation; all educators have known teachers who were skilled at their work in the classroom but who alienated their colleagues or who were unresponsive to parents. Such teachers are not complete professionals; their performance in these nonclassroom aspects of their practice should be strengthened so they can fully exhibit all the skills of effective teaching.

Discussion

Observations of practice other than classroom observations may be either formal or informal. If they are formal, they may be conducted in the same manner (with a planning conference, an observation, and a reflection conference) as a classroom observation. If informal, they don't include a planning conference, but they may be the subject of a reflection conference.

As noted, teachers do their work all day, every day, as they interact with students and other teachers in the corridors and as they attend meetings with colleagues. And, of course, as they work both formally and informally with students, teachers demonstrate and enhance their professionalism. It is absurd to think that one can assess teacher performance only by examining classroom behavior. Teaching is far more complex than that; everyday events provide opportunities for administrators, mentors, and coaches to help teachers become more thoughtful and reflective about all aspects of their practice.

Although it's true that professionalism is exhibited and developed in myriad ways, whether observations of practice other than classroom teaching may be used for formal teacher evaluation depends on the specific details of the negotiated agreement in each school district. However, a comprehensive approach to teacher evaluation will include such observations of practice simply because they demonstrate aspects of teaching that are not exhibited in any other manner.

When formulating a plan to include observations of practice into a comprehensive system of teacher evaluation and support, it is advisable for teachers and administrators to determine jointly which activities to include. For example, a teacher and an administrator might decide together that an important aspect of communicating with families consists of the presentation a teacher provides at back-to-school night, and they might agree that a supervisor will sit in on that session. Alternatively they might decide that a teacher's contributions during team or departmental meetings constitute an essential component of the teacher's interaction with colleagues (an element of Component 4d: Participating in a Professional Community); they could agree that a supervisor would sit in on some of those.

But even if observations of practice are not part of a formal approach to comprehensive teacher evaluation, teachers engage in these activities every day, and they are part of the teacher's professional persona. As such, they are worthy of note and comment and support in the ongoing effort to strengthen practice.

Procedures

1. If a teacher and an administrator have agreed upon a formal observation of a nonclassroom aspect of practice, conduct a preconference (planning conference), using questions similar to those used in a planning conference for a lesson:

- What do you hope to achieve (in this parent conference or this meeting with your department)?
- Describe the situation that leads you to work toward this outcome.
- What specific plans do you have for achieving your purpose?

2. Conduct the observation, either formally or informally. If this is a formal observation of practice, it should occur at the agreed-upon time, and the observer should take notes of what happens. If it is informal, it can occur at any time during the day, in the normal course of school events; note-taking by the observer is optional.

3. If the observation of practice is formal, conduct a postconference (reflection conference), using questions like those used in the reflection conference for a classroom observation:

- Did this meeting (parent conference, presentation) proceed as you expected? If not, what surprised you?
- Were you able to accomplish what you had hoped to accomplish during this meeting (parent conference, presentation)? How do you know?
- If you had an opportunity to conduct this meeting (parent conference, presentation) again, what would you do differently?

4. Notes from the observation and conference may be entered, as desired, on Form E: *Informal Classroom Observations*, for informal observations of components in Domains 1, 2, and 3; or on Form H: *Evidence for Domain 4*, for evidence collected in either formal or informal observations of components in Domain 4.

Examination of Artifacts

As noted in Chapter 1, artifacts provide the only evidence of certain aspects of teaching. For other aspects, they can supplement the evidence from observations of both classroom and nonclassroom practice.

Purpose

Artifacts provide a critical window into teaching practice; they offer evidence of a teacher's skill that may only be hinted at through observation. Thus the primary purpose of the examination of artifacts is to analyze material that reflects a teacher's skill in the many aspects of practice that are not directly observable. These artifacts become an integral part of the picture of a teacher's practice that may be used for evaluation or for mentoring and coaching to improve teaching.

Discussion

Conversations about artifacts (like conversations before and after an observation) encourage teachers to think deeply about what they do and why, and to analyze their practice against the components of the framework for teaching. Thus the collection and analysis of artifacts offer an opportunity for the activities known to promote professional learning: self-assessment, reflection on practice, and professional conversation.

As described in Chapter 1, artifacts provide the best—and in some cases the only—evidence for many of the behind-the-scenes aspects of teaching, particularly in Domain 1 (Planning and Preparation) and Domain 4 (Professional Responsibilities). A teacher's skill in communicating with families or a teacher's commitment to ongoing professional learning is simply not observable in the classroom. Thus if teachers are to demonstrate their skill in all aspects of teaching, it is important to supplement observations of classroom teaching and observations of other practice with the collection and examination of artifacts. Using a unit plan, for example, a teacher can demonstrate skill in long-range planning; similarly, a series of class newsletters indicate a teacher's approach to communicating with families.

But the examination of artifacts is important not only for discussion of behind-the-scenes aspects of teaching; it also can shed important light on the daily events of classroom teaching. For example, an assignment may be analyzed for its level of intellectual rigor. Some critical questions to be considered when looking at a student assignment or directions for an activity are "What are the students being asked to do? What is the cognitive level of this activity, and does this represent an appropriate mental stretch for these students?" This is not to suggest that low-level drill and practice should never be part of the teaching repertoire, but a steady diet of assignments that ask students to "fill in the blanks" or "answer the questions at the end of the chapter" can be deadly. Students become far more engaged in activities that ask them to draw their own conclusions, to formulate hypotheses, to analyze information. As they do those tasks they may have to read the chapter, and they will certainly acquire facts and concepts; but the *work*, from their point of view, requires considering an interesting question or solving a problem or puzzle.

Furthermore, as part of the artifact *Activity or Assignment* (see Appendix B), teachers are asked to collect samples of student work, representing the range of skill levels in their class. These samples may be the stimulus for much important conversation about practice, particularly if the assignment itself has been designed to reveal student understanding (or lack of it). First, one can easily discern whether or not the students have taken the assignment seriously. Next, and most important, if students have been asked to explain their answers, they reveal fascinating insights into their thought processes and their degree of understanding. This is critical information for teachers and provides an essential stimulus for reflection on practice and future planning.

Appendix B contains guidelines and forms for the collection of a number of artifacts. These artifacts are designed to provide evidence of a teacher's skill in many of the components in the framework for teaching.

Procedures

1. Determine, with the teacher, which artifacts are to be collected. For non-tenured teachers, the number and range of these artifacts should be limited in consideration of the heavy workload and steep learning curve experienced by many new teachers.

2. Schedule a conference to discuss the artifacts. When teachers know in advance which artifacts they are expected to assemble, and where the conference will be held, they can be prepared and the entire system is transparent.

Furthermore, particularly with experienced teachers, there is no reason why such artifact conferences must be one-on-one with an administrator; when teachers engage in a joint conference around artifacts, they have the opportunity to learn from one another.

Annual Evaluation

The annual evaluation represents the judgment that is made each year about a teacher's overall performance. It can take many forms, and the actual instrument used may be part of the district's negotiated agreement with its teachers union. Alternatively, the form itself may be established by state statute, and its use may be required by law.

Purpose

An annual evaluation fulfills a school district's legal obligation to declare, on an annual basis, that a teacher at least meets the district's minimum standard for performance.

Discussion

The issues involved in conducting an annual evaluation are presented at length in Chapters 4 and 5. Three main points are summarized here.

First, the evaluation decision is best conducted only as a dichotomous judgment ("does not meet" or "meets or exceeds" expectations.) For the vast majority of teachers whose performance meets or exceeds expectations, this practice has the consequence of shifting the attention of both teachers and administrators from the issues surrounding the ratings to those surrounding formative assessment and professional growth. In the rare cases in which a teacher's overall performance "does not meet" expectations, the instruments and procedures can help to identify and analyze areas for future learning.

Second, if the annual evaluation is based on ratings of performance, these ratings should be only at the level of the domain rather than for each individual component of the framework for teaching. As with the dichotomous judgment, this has the consequence of limiting discussion to the bigger picture of practice and to the identification of areas for learning.

Third, the performance of teachers engaged in self-directed professional inquiry may be evaluated according to whether they "do not meet" or "meet or exceed" expectations. But the expectations in this case do not refer to levels of performance in teaching. Rather they refer to the teacher's commitment to the process of inquiry and professional growth. As long as a teacher engages seriously in the process of professional learning and participates fully in the school's culture of inquiry, the criteria for these "other years" in the evaluation cycle would have been met.

Procedures

Two variations on completing the annual evaluation are presented here. The choice of which variation to follow depends on whether teacher performance has been rated on each domain as part of the process of classroom observation. If ratings have been assigned for each observation and transferred to Form M: *Summary of Observations and Artifacts*, the evaluator has, at the end of the year, an "at a glance" view of the teacher's performance. But not everyone favors that approach; some educators prefer to use Form G: *Formal Observation Summary* only for formative assessment and conversation, without assigning ratings. The following lists cover procedures for both variations.

Option 1: To be used if the level of performance on each domain has been determined as part of each formal observation, on the informal observations taken as a whole, and on the examination of artifacts.

1. Look at Form M: *Summary of Observations and Artifacts* and determine the patterns displayed. Be attentive not only to patterns across the four domains but also to demonstrations of growth over the year.

Note: While examining this form, pay particular attention to the circumstances surrounding each of the observations. For example, was the teacher attempting a new activity? Is the teacher new to this assignment?

2. Summarize the teacher's performance in each of the four domains of the framework for teaching; note these on the form.

3. Determine the teacher's general areas of strength and areas for further development; describe these on the Form N: *Annual Evaluation 1*.

4. Determine whether the teacher's performance "does not meet" or "meets or exceeds" the school's or district's expectations; indicate this at the bottom of the form.

5. Conduct an evaluation conference with the teacher to discuss these matters and to determine areas for further development. This discussion may provide guidance for the teacher in selecting growth goals for the following year.

6. Sign Form N and ask the teacher to do the same, indicating that the teacher has read the form.

Option 2: To be used if ratings have not been assigned following each formal observation, on the informal observations taken as a whole, and on the examination of artifacts.

1. Examine Form G: *Formal Observation Summary* for each of the observations conducted and any notes you have written on Form E: *Informal Classroom Observations.*

2. Summarize the teacher's performance in each of the four domains of the framework for teaching; note these on Form O: *Annual Evaluation 2.*

3. Determine the teacher's general areas for further development; briefly describe these on the form.

4. Determine whether the teacher's performance "does not meet" or "meets or exceeds" the school's or district's expectations; indicate this on the form.

5. Conduct an evaluation conference with the teacher to discuss these matters and to determine areas for further development. This discussion may provide guidance for the teacher in selecting growth goals for the following year.

6. Sign Form O and ask the teacher to do the same, indicating that the teacher has read the form.

✳ ✳ ✳ ✳ ✳

The recommended procedures offered in this chapter represent the collective wisdom of hundreds of educators around the world who have used the framework for teaching for a wide variety of purposes. Although educators may find that their local conditions warrant modifying the approaches suggested here, they should be aware that these recommendations are the result of a great deal of experience.

More important, however, the procedures represent a serious effort to engage teachers in the activities known to promote professional learning—namely, self-assessment, reflection on practice, and professional conversation, all conducted in an environment of trust. It is through this mechanism that the twin goals of teacher support—quality assurance and professional learning—can be achieved.

Appendix A: Instruments to Support Teacher Evaluation and Professional Learning

The forms in this appendix are designed to capture evidence of teaching in a way that maximizes the likelihood that teachers will find professional value in the experience. That is, the procedures for capturing evidence, as structured by the forms, encourage self-assessment, reflection on practice, and professional conversation—all of which contribute to teachers' professional learning. Everyone involved (teacher, mentor, coach, or evaluator) is likely to find the activities highly rewarding. As educators report, "It's all about the conversation."

When appraising performance, administrators must find ways to capture evidence of all components of the framework for teaching. This effort requires a combination of observations of teaching (both formal and informal), planning and reflection conferences, observations of other aspects of practice, and examination of artifacts.

In addition to being used for performance appraisal, the instruments provided here may be used for mentoring or coaching; but in that case, because no judgments are being made, it is not important to elicit evidence of all the components of the framework. Rather, the decisions about which instruments and procedures to use (whether it is observations of classroom practice, discussions of a unit plan, or the examination of an instructional artifact and an analysis of student work) are a matter for the educators involved to determine, based on the most important areas for focus.

The observation instruments may be used for either a general needs assessment or for a more structured examination of practice. A beginning teacher might ask a mentor to conduct a general observation or to examine some student work, with the aim of determining the areas of practice most in need of attention. Alternatively, a teacher—either a novice or a veteran—might ask an observer to concentrate on some specific aspect of teaching, such as the nature of the student interactions or the quality of the classroom discussion.

To help readers quickly find the instrument that will best suit their purpose, here is a list of the instruments with information about their uses and other explanatory comments.

Form A: Teacher Preparation Audit

• For teacher educators to determine where in their preparation programs students have an opportunity to learn about the components and common themes of the framework for teaching.

Comments: Teacher preparation programs attempt to teach their students everything they need to know about teaching—a daunting prospect. This audit provides teacher educators with a sense of how well they are achieving their aim.

Form B: Clinical Observation Notes

• For teachers-in-training to use in observing experienced teachers.
• For novice teachers to use in observing experienced teachers, as part of a mentoring program.

Comments: Using this form focuses the attention of the teacher-in-training and the novice teacher on specific aspects of the experienced teacher's practice.

Form C: Teaching Interview

• For teachers-in-training to use in conducting conversations with experienced teachers.
• For school district personnel to use in recruiting teachers for positions in their schools.
• For novice teachers to use in interviewing experienced teachers, as part of a mentoring program.
• To serve as the basis of a conversation between experienced teachers and administrators during the comprehensive evaluation phase of teacher evaluation.

Comments: These questions can reveal the rationale behind a teacher's actions, providing a window into the teacher's thinking.

Form D: Teacher Lesson Reflection

• For teachers-in-training to use in reflecting on lessons or lesson segments they have taught.
• For novice teachers to use as the basis for a conversation with mentors.
• For novice and experienced teachers to use as part of a formal observation process.

Comments: This form provides the structure for a critically important phase in the observation process; the act of structured reflection, based on evidence, contributes to professional learning.

Form E: Informal Classroom Observations
- For cooperating teachers to use while informally observing their student teachers.
- For mentors and coaches to use while observing the teachers with whom they are working.
- For administrators to use in the brief observations of practice they conduct throughout the school.

Comments: Informal observations may be brief and are likely to represent authentic and typical, rather than scripted, performance.

Form F: Formal Classroom Observation
- For cooperating teachers to use while formally observing their student teachers.
- For university supervisors to use while formally observing their student teachers.
- For administrators to use in conducting formal observations of teachers as part of a teacher evaluation process.

Comments: If possible, the notes from the lesson should be given to the teacher before the postconference (reflection conference), so the teacher can check them for accuracy.

Form G: Formal Observation Summary
- For cooperating teachers to use while formally observing their student teachers.
- For university supervisors to use while formally observing their student teachers.
- For administrators to use in conducting formal observations of teachers as part of a teacher evaluation process.

Comments: This form is the cornerstone of the formal observation, enabling observers and teachers to compare notes about their perceptions of a lesson and to determine together the lesson's strengths and the areas for growth. It can contribute to, but does not constitute, an evaluation of practice.

Form H: Evidence for Domain 4

- For use by teachers and administrators in identifying possible sources for the components in Domain 4.

Comments: A teacher's skill in Domain 4 is reflected in many different activities and artifacts; this form enables teachers and their mentors, coaches, or evaluators to identify those that are appropriate for a given situation.

Form I: Self-Assessment of Practice

- For experienced teachers in the first phase of Track 2 (self-directed professional inquiry), to engage in structured self-assessment on the components of the framework for teaching.

Comments: A teacher's goals for professional learning may derive from many sources, including general instructional strategies or a school's initiatives; however, a self-assessment can be the source of many important goals.

Form J: Individual Professional Development Plan

- For experienced teachers in the second phase of Track 2 (self-directed professional inquiry), to prepare a plan for how they will address their goals for professional learning.

Comments: This plan does not need to be elaborate, but it should be focused. If possible, it should include activities representing a variety of approaches: reading, attending workshops and conferences, talking with and observing colleagues, trying new practices in one's own classroom, inviting colleagues to observe and provide feedback.

Form K: Individual Professional Development Log of Activities

- For experienced teachers in the third phase of Track 2 (self-directed professional inquiry), to keep track of the activities they undertake for professional learning.

Comments: This log provides an important reminder of activities undertaken as part of the self-directed professional inquiry and makes the reflection and closure conference more meaningful.

Form L: Reflection on the Individual Professional Development Plan (IPDP)

- For experienced teachers in the final phase of Track 2 (self-directed professional inquiry), to reflect on the experience with their supervisor or colleagues.

Comments: Like an observation, the reflection on the process is the most important aspect of the self-directed inquiry for promoting professional learning. This reflection conference may be conducted with several teachers together; this practice has the enormous benefit of enabling teachers to learn from one another.

Form M: Summary of Observations and Artifacts
• (Optional) To provide a summary of a teacher's performance on the domains of the framework for teaching from formal observations, informal observations, and artifacts.

Comments: This form is used only if ratings have been given for teacher performance on each of the domains as a result of the formal and informal observations, and after an examination of artifacts. Using it has the advantage of enabling teachers, mentors and coaches, and supervisors to see patterns over time, as well as patterns of performance that might be obscured in the detail of observation reports.

Form N: Annual Evaluation 1
• To be used in verifying that a teacher's performance "meets or exceeds" (or, rarely, "does not meet") the district's expectations. It is used for Option 1 of the evaluation process.

Comments: Depending on statute and a district's negotiated agreement, this form (or its equivalent) may be the only documentation required for the annual evaluation of a teacher's performance. This form may be used for experienced teachers whether they are in the comprehensive phase or the self-directed inquiry phase of the evaluation system.

Form O: Annual Evaluation 2
• To be used in verifying that a teacher's performance "meets or exceeds" (or, rarely, "does not meet") the district's expectations. It is used for Option 2 of the evaluation process.

Comments: Depending on statute and a district's negotiated agreement, this form (or its equivalent) may be the only documentation required for the annual evaluation of a teacher's performance. This form may be used for experienced teachers whether they are in the comprehensive phase or the self-directed inquiry phase of the evaluation system.

Form A

Teacher Preparation Audit

Name of Preparation Program _____ Date _____

Component	Courses That Teach the Component	Comments
1a Demonstrating Knowledge of Content and Pedagogy		
1b Demonstrating Knowledge of Students		
1c Setting Instructional Outcomes		
1d Demonstrating Knowledge of Resources		
1e Designing Coherent Instruction		
1f Designing Student Assessments		
2a Creating an Environment of Respect and Rapport		
2b Establishing a Culture for Learning		
2c Managing Classroom Procedures		
2d Managing Student Behavior		
2e Organizing Physical Space		
3a Communicating with Students		
3b Using Questioning and Discussion Techniques		
3c Engaging Students in Learning		

(continued)

Form A—*Continued*

Component	Courses That Teach the Component	Comments
3d Using Assessment in Instruction		
3e Demonstrating Flexibility and Responsiveness		
4a Reflecting on Teaching		
4b Maintaining Accurate Records		
4c Communicating with Families		
4d Participating in a Professional Community		
4e Growing and Developing Professionally		
4f Showing Professionalism		
Equity		
High Expectations		
Cultural Competence		
Developmental Appropriateness		
Attention to Individual Students, Including Those with Special Needs		
Appropriate Use of Technology		
Student Assumption of Responsibility		

Form B
Clinical Observation Notes

Teacher _____ School _____

Grade Level(s) _____ Subject(s) _____ Date _____

Domain 1: Planning and Preparation

1a: Demonstrating Knowledge of Content and Pedagogy	The teacher demonstrates knowledge of the content and of the structure of the discipline, knowledge of prerequisite relationships, and common student misconceptions.
Evidence	
1b: Demonstrating Knowledge of Students	The teacher demonstrates familiarity with individual students' backgrounds, cultures, skills, language proficiency, interests, and special needs.
Evidence	
1c: Setting Instructional Outcomes	The teacher's instructional purpose is clear, reflecting rigorous learning and curriculum standards. Different types of content are represented (e.g., knowledge, thinking skills).
Evidence	

(continued)

Form B—*Continued*

Domain 2: The Classroom Environment

2a: Creating an Environment of Respect and Rapport	Classroom interactions between the teacher and students are respectful, reflecting warmth and caring and sensitivity to students' cultures and levels of development. Student interactions are respectful.
Evidence	
2b: Establishing a Culture for Learning	The level of energy, from both students and teacher, is high, creating a culture for learning in which the subject is important and students clearly take pride in their work.
Evidence	
2c: Managing Classroom Procedures	Little instructional time is lost because of classroom routines and procedures, transitions, handling of supplies, and performance of noninstructional duties, which occur smoothly. Students contribute to classroom routines.
Evidence	
2d: Managing Student Behavior	Standards of conduct are clear, with teacher's sensitive monitoring of student behavior and subtle response to misbehavior.
Evidence	
2e: Organizing Physical Space	The classroom is safe, and the physical environment ensures the learning of all students and is conducive to the goals of the lesson. Technology is used skillfully, as appropriate to the lesson.
Evidence	

Domain 3: Instruction

3a: Communicating with Students	Expectations for learning, directions, and procedures are clear to students. The teacher's explanation of content is effective and anticipates possible student misconceptions.
Evidence	

3b: Using Questioning and Discussion Techniques	The teacher's questions are at a high cognitive level, and the teacher allows sufficient time for students to answer. All students participate in the discussion, with the teacher stepping aside when appropriate.
Evidence	

3c: Engaging Students in Learning	Students are engaged throughout the lesson in learning. The activities, student groupings, and materials are appropriate to the instructional outcomes. The lesson's structure is coherent, with suitable pace.
Evidence	

3d: Using Assessment in Instruction	Assessment is used in instruction, through self-assessment by students, monitoring of progress of learning by teacher and/or students, and high-quality feedback to students. Students are fully aware of the assessment criteria used to evaluate their work.
Evidence	

3e: Demonstrating Flexibility and Responsiveness	The teacher seizes an opportunity to enhance learning, building on a spontaneous event or student interests. The teacher adjusts the lesson when needed.
Evidence	

Form C
Teaching Interview (Annotated)

Teacher _____ School _____

Grade Level(s) _____ Subject(s) _____ Date _____

Questions for discussion

1. How did you become knowledgeable about the subjects you teach and about how best to teach those to students? (For example, a college major or minor, various workshops or training sessions) *This question asks teachers to comment on the level of their preparation in both content and pedagogy. (Component 1a)*

2. How do you stay abreast of the subjects you teach and of the current research on how best to teach them? (For example, attending courses and workshops, reading professional literature) *This question is intended to elicit teachers' commitment to ongoing learning in the different disciplines they teach, including evolving research on how best to teach those disciplines to students. (Component 4e)*

3. How do you become familiar with your students' skills and knowledge? (For example, diagnostic assessments, information from previous years' teachers) *This question is intended to find out about teachers' techniques in learning about their students' levels of proficiency in the curriculum. (Component 1b)*

4. How do you become familiar with your students' individual interests and cultural backgrounds? (For example, interest inventories, dialogue with parents, attendance at students' athletic events) *This question is intended to find out about teachers' techniques for learning about their students' out-of-school interests, talents, hobbies, family traditions, and so on. (Component 1b)*

5. Describe how you establish and implement important classroom routines and procedures. (For example, distribution and collection of materials, transitions between activities) *A smoothly running classroom is a hallmark of experience. This question invites teachers to describe how they establish such a classroom. (Component 2c)*

6. Describe how you establish and maintain standards of student conduct. (For example, determining and posting classroom expectations, conducting classroom meetings) *In a well-functioning classroom, students know the expectations for behavior and contribute to the positive tone of the class. (Component 2d)*

7. Describe how you establish and maintain an atmosphere of trust, openness, and mutual respect. (For example, model respectful language, recognize students who demonstrate respect) *When adults recall their school experiences years later, the most powerful memories concern how they were treated by teachers and other students. (Component 2a)*

8. What resources (people, materials, community resources) are available to you in planning instruction or for classroom use? (For example, museums, local experts, videos, print materials, Web sites) *The use of outside resources enriches the learning experiences teachers design for students. Awareness of those resources enables a teacher to go beyond textbooks and other classroom materials. (Component 1d)*

9. What resources (people, materials, programs) are available to your students if they need assistance? (For example, big brother/sister programs, clothing donations, counseling resources) *Some students need physical objects (for example, winter coats) or support services (for example, counseling). Every teacher, in addition to being alert to such needs, should know where to locate such resources. (Component 1d)*

10. Describe how you use your physical setting to maximize student learning. (For example, chairs in a circle for discussion; desks pushed into "tables" for science activities; visually impaired students at the front) *This question is intended to elicit a teacher's approach to the use of physical space. Of course, some teachers, such as those who share a room or who work from a cart, have little control over their teaching space. (Component 2e)*

11. How do you encourage your students to assume responsibility for their learning? (For example, inviting students to share their thinking, asking students for their ideas regarding a proposed approach to learning a concept) *The active involvement of students in the classroom environment is a characteristic of the distinguished level of performance in many of the components of the framework for teaching. (Many components)*

12. Describe how you incorporate the use of electronic technology into your practice. (For example, finding materials for students, maintaining records of student progress, putting student assignments on the school's Web site) *Electronic technology infuses many aspects of a teacher's practice; many teachers actively strive to increase their use of these powerful approaches. Appropriate use of technology is reflected in many components of the framework.*

13. How do you coordinate learning activities with other colleagues? (For example, same grade level, same content, special education or language acquisition teachers) *This question elicits information about a teacher's participation in a professional learning community. (Component 4d)*

Form C

Teaching Interview

Teacher _____ School _____

Grade Level(s) _____ Subject(s) _____ Date _____

Questions for discussion:

1. How did you become knowledgeable about the subjects you teach and about how best to teach those to students? (For example, a college major or minor, various workshops or training sessions)

2. How do you stay abreast of the subjects you teach and of the current research on how best to teach them? (For example, attending courses and workshops, reading professional literature)

3. How do you become familiar with your students' skills and knowledge? (For example, diagnostic assessments, information from previous years' teachers)

4. How do you become familiar with your students' individual interests and cultural backgrounds? (For example, interest inventories, dialogue with parents, attendance at students' athletic events)

5. Describe how you establish and implement important classroom routines and procedures. (For example, distribution and collection of materials, transitions between activities)

6. Describe how you establish and maintain standards of student conduct. (For example, determining and posting classroom expectations, conducting classroom meetings)

7. Describe how you establish and maintain an atmosphere of trust, openness, and mutual respect. (For example, model respectful language, recognize students who demonstrate respect)

8. What resources (people, materials, community resources) are available to you in planning instruction or for classroom use? (For example, museums, local experts, videos, print materials, Web sites)

9. What resources (people, materials, programs) are available to your students if they need assistance? (For example, big brother/sister programs, clothing donations, counseling resources)

10. Describe how you use your physical setting to maximize student learning. (For example, chairs in a circle for discussion; desks pushed into "tables" for science activities; visually impaired students at the front)

11. How do you encourage your students to assume responsibility for their learning? (For example, inviting students to share their thinking, asking students for their ideas regarding a proposed approach to learning a concept)

12. Describe how you incorporate the use of electronic technology into your practice. (For example, finding materials for students, maintaining records of student progress, putting student assignments on the school's Web site)

13. How do you coordinate learning activities with other colleagues? (For example, same grade level, same content, special education or language acquisition teachers)

Form D
Teacher Lesson Reflection

Name _____ School _____ Date _____

1. In general, how successful was the lesson? Did the students learn what you intended for them to learn? How do you know?

2. If you have samples of student work, what do they reveal about the students' levels of engagement and understanding? Do they suggest modifications in how you might teach this lesson in the future?

3. Comment on your classroom procedures, student conduct, and your use of physical space. To what extent did these contribute to student learning?

4. Did you depart from your plan? If so, how and why?

5. Comment on different aspects of your instructional delivery (e.g., activities, grouping of students, materials, and resources). To what extent were they effective?

6. If you had an opportunity to teach this lesson again to the same group of students, what would you do differently?

7. Consider different aspects of your planning and execution of the lesson in light of the domains and components on the following pages. Determine evidence, if any, for each of the components, and what that evidence demonstrates about your level of performance.

(continued)

Form D—*Continued*
Domain 1: Planning and Preparation

Component	Unsatisfactory	Basic	Proficient	Distinguished
1a Demonstrating Knowledge of Content and Pedagogy	The teacher's plans and practice display little knowledge of content, prerequisite relationships between different aspects of the content, or the instructional practices specific to that discipline.	The teacher's plans and practice reflect some awareness of the important concepts in the discipline, prerequisite relationships between them, and the instructional practices specific to that discipline.	The teacher's plans and practice reflect solid knowledge of the content, prerequisite relationships between important concepts, and the instructional practices specific to that discipline.	The teacher's plans and practice reflect extensive knowledge of the content and the structure of the discipline. The teacher actively builds on knowledge of prerequisites and misconceptions when describing instruction or seeking causes for student misunderstanding.
Evidence				

Component	Unsatisfactory	Basic	Proficient	Distinguished
1b Demonstrating Knowledge of Students	The teacher demonstrates little or no knowledge of students' backgrounds, cultures, skills, language proficiency, interests, and special needs, and does not seek such understanding.	The teacher indicates the importance of understanding students' backgrounds, cultures, skills, language proficiency, interests, and special needs, and attains this knowledge for the class as a whole.	The teacher actively seeks knowledge of students' backgrounds, cultures, skills, language proficiency, interests, and special needs, and attains this knowledge for groups of students.	The teacher actively seeks knowledge of students' backgrounds, cultures, skills, language proficiency, interests, and special needs from a variety of sources, and attains this knowledge for individual students.
Evidence				

Component	Unsatisfactory	Basic	Proficient	Distinguished
1c **Setting Instructional Outcomes**	Instructional outcomes are unsuitable for students, represent trivial or low-level learning, or are stated only as activities. They do not permit viable methods of assessment.	Instructional outcomes are of moderate rigor and are suitable for some students, but consist of a combination of activities and goals, some of which permit viable methods of assessment. They reflect more than one type of learning, but the teacher makes no attempt at coordination or integration.	Instructional outcomes are stated as goals reflecting high-level learning and curriculum standards. They are suitable for most students in the class, represent different types of learning, and can be assessed. The outcomes reflect opportunities for coordination.	Instructional outcomes are stated as goals that can be assessed, reflecting rigorous learning and curriculum standards. They represent different types of content, offer opportunities for both coordination and integration, and take account of the needs of individual students.

Evidence

Component	Unsatisfactory	Basic	Proficient	Distinguished
1d **Demonstrating Knowledge of Resources**	The teacher demonstrates little or no familiarity with resources to enhance own knowledge, to use in teaching, or for students who need them. The teacher does not seek such knowledge.	The teacher demonstrates some familiarity with resources available through the school or district to enhance own knowledge, to use in teaching, or for students who need them. The teacher does not seek to extend such knowledge.	The teacher is fully aware of the resources available through the school or district to enhance own knowledge, to use in teaching, or for students who need them.	The teacher seeks out resources in and beyond the school or district in professional organizations, on the Internet, and in the community to enhance own knowledge, to use in teaching, and for students who need them.

Evidence

(continued)

Form D—*Continued*

Component	Unsatisfactory	Basic	Proficient	Distinguished
1e **Designing Coherent Instruction**	The series of learning experiences is poorly aligned with the instructional outcomes and does not represent a coherent structure. The experiences are suitable for only some students.	The series of learning experiences demonstrates partial alignment with instructional outcomes, and some of the experiences are likely to engage students in significant learning. The lesson or unit has a recognizable structure and reflects partial knowledge of students and resources.	The teacher coordinates knowledge of content, of students, and of resources to design a series of learning experiences aligned to instructional outcomes and suitable for groups of students. The lesson or unit has a clear structure and is likely to engage students in significant learning.	The teacher coordinates knowledge of content, of students, and of resources to design a series of learning experiences aligned to instructional outcomes, differentiated where appropriate to make them suitable for all students, and likely to engage them in significant learning. The lesson or unit structure is clear and allows for different pathways according to student needs.

Evidence

Component	Unsatisfactory	Basic	Proficient	Distinguished
1f **Designing Student Assessments**	The teacher's plan for assessing student learning contains no clear criteria or standards, is poorly aligned with the instructional outcomes, or is inappropriate for many students. The results of assessment have minimal impact on the design of future instruction.	The teacher's plan for student assessment is partially aligned with the instructional outcomes, without clear criteria, and inappropriate for at least some students. The teacher intends to use assessment results to plan for future instruction for the class as a whole.	The teacher's plan for student assessment is aligned with the instructional outcomes, uses clear criteria, and is appropriate to the needs of students. The teacher intends to use assessment results to plan for future instruction for groups of students.	The teacher's plan for student assessment is fully aligned with the instructional outcomes, with clear criteria and standards that show evidence of student contributions to their development. Assessment methodologies may have been adapted for individuals, and the teacher intends to use assessment results to plan future instruction for individual students.

Evidence

Domain 2: The Classroom Environment

Component	Unsatisfactory	Basic	Proficient	Distinguished
2a Creating an Environment of Respect and Rapport	Classroom interactions, both between the teacher and students and among students, are negative, inappropriate, or insensitive to students' cultural backgrounds and are characterized by sarcasm, put-downs, or conflict.	Classroom interactions, both between the teacher and students and among students, are generally appropriate and free from conflict but may be characterized by occasional displays of insensitivity or lack of responsiveness to cultural or developmental differences among students.	Classroom interactions between the teacher and students and among students are polite and respectful, reflecting general warmth and caring, and are appropriate to the cultural and developmental differences among groups of students.	Classroom interactions between the teacher and individual students are highly respectful, reflecting genuine warmth and caring and sensitivity to students' cultures and levels of development. Students themselves ensure high levels of civility among members of the class.
Evidence				

Component	Unsatisfactory	Basic	Proficient	Distinguished
2b Establishing a Culture for Learning	The classroom environment conveys a negative culture for learning, characterized by low teacher commitment to the subject, low expectations for student achievement, and little or no student pride in work.	The teacher's attempt to create a culture for learning is partially successful, with little teacher commitment to the subject, modest expectations for student achievement, and little student pride in work. Both teacher and students appear to be only "going through the motions."	The classroom culture is characterized by high expectations for most students and genuine commitment to the subject by both teacher and students, with students demonstrating pride in their work.	High levels of student energy and teacher passion for the subject create a culture for learning in which everyone shares a belief in the importance of the subject and all students hold themselves to high standards of performance—for example, by initiating improvements to their work.
Evidence				

(continued)

Form D—Continued

Component	Unsatisfactory	Basic	Proficient	Distinguished
2c Managing Classroom Procedures	Much instructional time is lost because of inefficient classroom routines and procedures for transitions, handling of supplies, and performance of noninstructional duties.	Some instructional time is lost because classroom routines and procedures for transitions, handling of supplies, and performance of noninstructional duties are only partially effective.	Little instructional time is lost because of classroom routines and procedures for transitions, handling of supplies, and performance of noninstructional duties, which occur smoothly.	Students contribute to the seamless operation of classroom routines and procedures for transitions, handling of supplies, and performance of noninstructional duties.

Evidence

Component	Unsatisfactory	Basic	Proficient	Distinguished
2d Managing Student Behavior	There is no evidence that standards of conduct have been established and little or no teacher monitoring of student behavior. Response to student misbehavior is repressive or disrespectful of student dignity.	It appears that the teacher has made an effort to establish standards of conduct for students. The teacher tries, with uneven results, to monitor student behavior and respond to student misbehavior.	Standards of conduct appear to be clear to students, and the teacher monitors student behavior against those standards. The teacher's response to student misbehavior is appropriate and respects the students' dignity.	Standards of conduct are clear, with evidence of student participation in setting them. The teacher's monitoring of student behavior is subtle and preventive, and the teacher's response to student misbehavior is sensitive to individual student needs. Students take an active role in monitoring the standards of behavior.

Evidence

Component	Unsatisfactory	Basic	Proficient	Distinguished
2e Organizing Physical Space	The physical environment is unsafe, or some students don't have access to learning. Alignment between the physical arrangement and the lesson activities is poor.	The classroom is safe, and essential learning is accessible to most students; the teacher's use of physical resources, including computer technology, is moderately effective. The teacher may attempt to modify the physical arrangement to suit learning activities, with partial success.	The classroom is safe, and learning is accessible to all students; the teacher ensures that the physical arrangement is appropriate to the learning activities. The teacher makes effective use of physical resources, including computer technology.	The classroom is safe, and the physical environment ensures the learning of all students, including those with special needs. Students contribute to the use or adaptation of the physical environment to advance learning. Technology is used skillfully, as appropriate to the lesson.
Evidence				

Domain 3: Instruction

Component	Unsatisfactory	Basic	Proficient	Distinguished
3a Communicating with Students	Expectations for learning, directions and procedures, and explanations of content are unclear or confusing to students. The teacher's use of language contains errors or is inappropriate for students' cultures or levels of development.	Expectations for learning, directions and procedures, and explanations of content are clarified after initial confusion; the teacher's use of language is correct but may not be completely appropriate for students' cultures or levels of development.	Expectations for learning, directions and procedures, and explanations of content are clear to students. Communications are appropriate for students' cultures and levels of development.	Expectations for learning, directions and procedures, and explanations of content are clear to students. The teacher's oral and written communication is clear and expressive, appropriate for students' cultures and levels of development, and anticipates possible student misconceptions.
Evidence				

(continued)

Form D—*Continued*

Component	Unsatisfactory	Basic	Proficient	Distinguished
3b Using Questioning and Discussion Techniques	The teacher's questions are low-level or inappropriate, eliciting limited student participation and recitation rather than discussion.	Some of the teacher's questions elicit a thoughtful response, but most are low-level, posed in rapid succession. The teacher's attempts to engage all students in the discussion are only partially successful.	Most of the teacher's questions elicit a thoughtful response, and the teacher allows sufficient time for students to answer. All students participate in the discussion, with the teacher stepping aside when appropriate.	Questions reflect high expectations and are culturally and developmentally appropriate. Students formulate many of the high-level questions and ensure that all voices are heard.

Evidence

Component	Unsatisfactory	Basic	Proficient	Distinguished
3c Engaging Students in Learning	Activities and assignments, materials, and groupings of students are inappropriate for the instructional outcomes or students' cultures or levels of understanding, resulting in little intellectual engagement. The lesson has no structure or is poorly paced.	Activities and assignments, materials, and groupings of students are partially appropriate for the instructional outcomes or students' cultures or levels of understanding, resulting in moderate intellectual engagement. The lesson has a recognizable structure, but that structure is not fully maintained.	Activities and assignments, materials, and groupings of students are fully appropriate for the instructional outcomes and students' cultures and levels of understanding. All students are engaged in work of a high level of rigor. The lesson's structure is coherent, with appropriate pace.	Students, throughout the lesson, are highly intellectually engaged in significant learning and make material contributions to the activities, student groupings, and materials. The lesson is adapted as necessary to the needs of individuals, and the structure and pacing allow for student reflection and closure.

Evidence

Component	Unsatisfactory	Basic	Proficient	Distinguished
3d **Using Assessment in Instruction**	Assessment is not used in instruction, either through monitoring of progress by the teacher or students, or through feedback to students. Students are unaware of the assessment criteria used to evaluate their work.	Assessment is occasionally used in instruction, through some monitoring of progress of learning by the teacher and/or students. Feedback to students is uneven, and students are aware of only some of the assessment criteria used to evaluate their work.	Assessment is regularly used in instruction, through self-assessment by students, monitoring of progress of learning by the teacher and/or students, and high-quality feedback to students. Students are fully aware of the assessment criteria used to evaluate their work.	Assessment is used in a sophisticated manner in instruction, through student involvement in establishing the assessment criteria, self-assessment by students, monitoring of progress by both students and teachers, and high-quality feedback to students from a variety of sources.

Evidence

Component	Unsatisfactory	Basic	Proficient	Distinguished
3e **Demonstrating Flexibility and Responsiveness**	The teacher adheres to the instruction plan, even when a change would improve the lesson or address students' lack of interest. The teacher brushes aside student questions; when students experience difficulty, the teacher blames the students or their home environment.	The teacher attempts to modify the lesson when needed and to respond to student questions, with moderate success. The teacher accepts responsibility for student success, but has only a limited repertoire of strategies to draw upon.	The teacher promotes the successful learning of all students, making adjustments as needed to instruction plans and accommodating student questions, needs, and interests.	The teacher seizes an opportunity to enhance learning, building on a spontaneous event or student interests. The teacher ensures the success of all students, using an extensive repertoire of instructional strategies.

Evidence

Form E
Informal Classroom Observations

Teacher _____ School _____

Grade Level(s) _____ Subject(s) _____ Observer _____

Date	Topic, Concept, Setting

(continued)

Domain 1: Planning and Preparation

Form E—*Continued*

Component	Unsatisfactory	Basic	Proficient	Distinguished
1a Demonstrating Knowledge of Content and Pedagogy	The teacher's plans and practice display little knowledge of the content, prerequisite relationships between different aspects of the content, or the instructional practices specific to that discipline.	The teacher's plans and practice reflect some awareness of the important concepts in the discipline, prerequisite relationships between them, and the instructional practices specific to that discipline.	The teacher's plans and practice reflect solid knowledge of the content, prerequisite relationships between important concepts, and the instructional practices specific to that discipline.	The teacher's plans and practice reflect extensive knowledge of the content and the structure of the discipline. The teacher actively builds on knowledge of prerequisites and misconceptions when describing instruction or seeking causes for student misunderstanding.

Evidence
Date:
Date:
Date:

Component	Unsatisfactory	Basic	Proficient	Distinguished
1b Demonstrating Knowledge of Students	The teacher demonstrates little or no knowledge of students' backgrounds, cultures, skills, language proficiency, interests, and special needs, and does not seek such understanding.	The teacher indicates the importance of understanding students' backgrounds, cultures, skills, language proficiency, interests, and special needs, and attains this knowledge for the class as a whole.	The teacher actively seeks knowledge of students' backgrounds, cultures, skills, language proficiency, interests, and special needs, and attains this knowledge for groups of students.	The teacher actively seeks knowledge of students' backgrounds, cultures, skills, language proficiency, interests, and special needs from a variety of sources, and attains this knowledge for individual students.

Evidence
Date:
Date:
Date:

Form E—*Continued*

Domain 2: The Classroom Environment

Component	Unsatisfactory	Basic	Proficient	Distinguished
2a Creating an Environment of Respect and Rapport	Classroom interactions, both between the teacher and students and among students, are negative, inappropriate, or insensitive to students' cultural backgrounds and are characterized by sarcasm, put-downs, or conflict.	Classroom interactions, both between the teacher and students and among students, are generally appropriate and free from conflict, but may be characterized by occasional displays of insensitivity or lack of responsiveness to cultural or developmental differences among students.	Classroom interactions, both between the teacher and students and among students, are polite and respectful, reflecting general warmth and caring, and are appropriate to the cultural and developmental differences among groups of students.	Classroom interactions among the teacher and individual students are highly respectful, reflecting genuine warmth and caring and sensitivity to students' cultures and levels of development. Students themselves ensure high levels of civility among members of the class.

Evidence
Date:
Date:
Date:

Component	Unsatisfactory	Basic	Proficient	Distinguished
2b Establishing a Culture for Learning	The classroom environment conveys a negative culture for learning, characterized by low teacher commitment to the subject, low expectations for student achievement, and little or no student pride in work.	The teacher's attempt to create a culture for learning is partially successful, with little teacher commitment to the subject, modest expectations for student achievement, and little student pride in work. Both teacher and students appear to be only "going through the motions."	The classroom culture is characterized by high expectations for most students and genuine commitment to the subject by both teacher and students, with students demonstrating pride in their work.	High levels of student energy and teacher passion for the subject create a culture of learning in which everyone shares a belief in the importance of the subject and all students hold themselves to high standards of performance—for example, by initiating improvements to their work.

Evidence
Date:
Date:
Date:

Component	Unsatisfactory	Basic	Proficient	Distinguished
2c Managing Classroom Procedures	Classroom routines and procedures for transitions, handling of supplies, and performance of noninstructional duties are either nonexistent or inefficient, resulting in the loss of much instructional time.	Classroom routines and procedures for transitions, handling of supplies, and performance of noninstructional duties have been established but function unevenly or inconsistently, with some loss of instructional time.	Classroom routines and procedures for transitions, handling of supplies, and performance of noninstructional duties have been established and function smoothly, with little loss of instructional time.	Classroom routines and procedures for transitions, handling of supplies, and performance of noninstructional duties are seamless in their operation, with students assuming considerable responsibility for their smooth functioning.

Evidence
Date:
Date:
Date:

Component	Unsatisfactory	Basic	Proficient	Distinguished
2d Managing Student Behavior	There is no evidence that standards of conduct have been established and little or no teacher monitoring of student behavior. Response to student misbehavior is repressive or disrespectful of student dignity.	It appears that the teacher has made an effort to establish standards of conduct for students and tries to monitor student behavior and respond to student misbehavior, but these efforts are not always successful.	Standards of conduct appear to be clear to students, and the teacher monitors student behavior against those standards. The teacher's response to student misbehavior is appropriate and respectful to students.	Standards of conduct are clear, with evidence of student participation in setting them. The teacher's monitoring of student behavior is subtle and preventive, and the teacher's response to student misbehavior is sensitive to individual student needs. Students take an active role in monitoring the standards of behavior.

Evidence
Date:
Date:
Date:

(continued)

Form E—*Continued*

Component	Unsatisfactory	Basic	Proficient	Distinguished	
2e Organizing Physical Space	The teacher makes poor use of the physical environment, resulting in unsafe or inaccessible conditions for some students or a significant mismatch between the physical arrangement and the lesson activities.	The classroom is safe, and essential learning is accessible to most students, but the physical arrangement only partially supports the learning activities. The teacher's use of physical resources, including computer technology, is moderately effective.	The classroom is safe, and learning is accessible to all students; the teacher ensures that the physical arrangement supports the learning activities. The teacher makes effective use of physical resources, including computer technology.	The classroom is safe, and the physical environment ensures the learning of all students, including those with special needs. Students contribute to the use or adaptation of the physical environment to advance learning. Technology is used skillfully, as appropriate to the lesson.	
Evidence *Date:* *Date:* *Date:*					

Domain 3: Instruction

Component	Unsatisfactory	Basic	Proficient	Distinguished	
3a Communicating with Students	The teacher's oral and written communication contains errors or is unclear or inappropriate to students' cultures or levels of development.	The teacher's oral and written communication contains no errors but may not be completely appropriate to students' cultures or levels of development. It may require further elaboration to avoid confusion.	The teacher communicates clearly and accurately to students, both orally and in writing. Communications are appropriate to students' cultures and levels of development.	The teacher's oral and written communication is clear and expressive, appropriate to students' cultures and levels of development. It also anticipates possible student misconceptions.	
Evidence *Date:* *Date:* *Date:*					

Component	Unsatisfactory	Basic	Proficient	Distinguished
3b Using Questioning and Discussion Techniques	The teacher makes poor use of questioning and discussion techniques, with low-level or inappropriate questions, limited student participation, and little true discussion.	The teacher's use of questioning and discussion techniques is uneven, with some high-level questions, attempts at true discussion, and moderate student participation.	The teacher' use of questioning and discussion techniques reflects high-level questions, true discussion, and participation by all students.	Questions reflect high expectations and are culturally and developmentally appropriate. Students formulate many of the high-level questions and assume the responsibility for the participation of all students in the discussion.

Evidence
Date:
Date:
Date:

Component	Unsatisfactory	Basic	Proficient	Distinguished
3c Engaging Students in Learning	Students are not at all intellectually engaged in learning, as a result of groupings, activities, or materials inappropriate to their cultures or levels of understanding, poor representations of content, or lack of lesson structure.	Students are intellectually engaged only partially in significant learning, as a result of groupings, activities, or materials culturally or developmentally appropriate to only some students, or uneven lesson structure or pacing.	Students are intellectually engaged throughout the lesson in significant learning, with appropriate groupings, activities, and materials, instructive presentations of content, and suitable lesson structure and pacing.	Students, throughout the lesson, are highly intellectually engaged in significant learning and make material contributions to the representation of content, the groupings, the activities, and the materials. The lesson is adapted as necessary to the needs of individuals, and the structure and pacing allow for student reflection and closure.

Evidence
Date:
Date:
Date:

(continued)

Form E—*Continued*

Component	Unsatisfactory	Basic	Proficient	Distinguished
3d **Using** **Assessment in** **Instruction**	Assessment is not used in instruction, either through monitoring of progress by the teacher or students, or through feedback to students; students are unaware of the assessment criteria used to evaluate their work.	Assessment is occasionally used in instruction, through some monitoring of progress of learning by teacher and/or students. Feedback to students is uneven, and students are aware of only some of the assessment criteria used to evaluate their work.	Assessment is regularly used in instruction, through self-assessment by students, monitoring of progress of learning by teacher and/or students, and high-quality feedback to students. Students are fully aware of the assessment criteria used to evaluate their work.	Assessment is used in a sophisticated manner in instruction, through student involvement in establishing the assessment criteria, self-assessment by students and monitoring of progress by both students and teachers, and high-quality feedback to students from a variety of sources.

Evidence
Date:
Date:
Date:

Component	Unsatisfactory	Basic	Proficient	Distinguished
3e **Demonstrating** **Flexibility and** **Responsiveness**	The teacher adheres to the instruction plan in spite of evidence of poor student understanding or of students' lack of interest, and fails to respond to student questions; the teacher assumes no responsibility for students' failure to understand.	The teacher demonstrates moderate flexibility and responsiveness to student questions, needs, and interests during a lesson, and seeks to ensure the success of all students.	The teacher ensures the successful learning of all students, making adjustments as needed to instruction plans and responding to student questions, needs, and interests.	The teacher is highly responsive to individual students' needs, interests, and questions, making even major lesson adjustments as necessary to meet instructional goals, and persists in ensuring the success of all students.

Evidence
Date:
Date:
Date:

Form F

Formal Classroom Observation

Teacher _____ School _____

Grade Level(s) _____ Subject(s) _____

Observer _____ Date _____

Interview Protocol for a Preconference (Planning Conference)

Questions for discussion:

1. To which part of your curriculum does this lesson relate?

2. How does this learning fit in the sequence of learning for this class?

3. Briefly describe the students in this class, including those with special needs.

4. What are your learning outcomes for this lesson? What do you want the students to understand?

5. How will you engage the students in the learning? What will you do? What will the students do? Will the students work in groups, or individually, or as a large group? Provide any worksheets or other materials the students will be using.

6. How will you differentiate instruction for different individuals or groups of students in the class?

7. How and when will you know whether the students have learned what you intend?

8. Is there anything that you would like me to specifically observe during the lesson?

(continued)

Form F—*Continued*

Notes from the Observation

Time	Actions and Statements/Questions by Teacher and Students	Component

Interview Protocol for a Postconference (Reflection Conference)

Teacher _____ School _____

1. In general, how successful was the lesson? Did the students learn what you intended for them to learn? How do you know?

2. If you were able to bring samples of student work, what do those samples reveal about those students' levels of engagement and understanding?

3. Comment on your classroom procedures, student conduct, and your use of physical space. To what extent did these contribute to student learning?

4. Did you depart from your plan? If so, how and why?

5. Comment on different aspects of your instructional delivery (e.g., activities, grouping of students, materials and resources). To what extent were they effective?

6. If you had an opportunity to teach this lesson again to the same group of students, what would you do differently?

Form G

Formal Observation Summary

Teacher _____   Grade Level(s) _____

School _____

Subject(s) _____   Observer _____   Date _____

Summary of the Lesson _____

Evidence of Teaching

Domain 1: Planning and Preparation

Component	Unsatisfactory	Basic	Proficient	Distinguished
1a Demonstrating Knowledge of Content and Pedagogy	The teacher's plans and practice display little knowledge of the content, prerequisite relationships between different aspects of the content, or the instructional practices specific to that discipline.	The teacher's plans and practice reflect some awareness of the important concepts in the discipline, prerequisite relationships between them, and instructional practices specific to that discipline.	The teacher's plans and practice reflect solid knowledge of the content, prerequisite relationships between important concepts, and the instructional practices specific to that discipline.	The teacher's plans and practice reflect extensive knowledge of the content and the structure of the discipline. The teacher actively builds on knowledge of prerequisites and misconceptions when describing instruction or seeking causes for student misunderstanding.

Evidence

Component	Unsatisfactory	Basic	Proficient	Distinguished
1b Demonstrating Knowledge of Students	The teacher demonstrates little or no knowledge of students' backgrounds, cultures, skills, language proficiency, interests, and special needs, and does not seek such understanding.	The teacher indicates the importance of understanding students' backgrounds, cultures, skills, language proficiency, interests, and special needs, and attains this knowledge for the class as a whole.	The teacher actively seeks knowledge of students' backgrounds, cultures, skills, language proficiency, interests, and special needs, and attains this knowledge for groups of students.	The teacher actively seeks knowledge of students' backgrounds, cultures, skills, language proficiency, interests, and special needs from a variety of sources, and attains this knowledge for individual students.

Evidence

Component	Unsatisfactory	Basic	Proficient	Distinguished
Ic Setting Instructional Outcomes	Instructional outcomes are unsuitable for students, represent trivial or low-level learning, or are stated only as activities. They do not permit viable methods of assessment.	Instructional outcomes are of moderate rigor and are suitable for some students, but consist of a combination of activities and goals, some of which permit viable methods of assessment. They reflect more than one type of learning, but the teacher makes no attempt at coordination or integration.	Instructional outcomes are stated as goals reflecting high-level learning and curriculum standards. They are suitable for most students in the class, represent different types of learning, and can be assessed. The outcomes reflect opportunities for coordination.	Instructional outcomes are stated as goals that can be assessed, reflecting rigorous learning and curriculum standards. They represent different types of content, offer opportunities for both coordination and integration, and take account of the needs of individual students.

Evidence

Component	Unsatisfactory	Basic	Proficient	Distinguished
Id Demonstrating Knowledge of Resources	The teacher demonstrates little or no familiarity with resources to enhance own knowledge, to use in teaching, or for students who need them. The teacher does not seek such knowledge.	The teacher demonstrates some familiarity with resources available through the school or district to enhance own knowledge, to use in teaching, or for students who need them. The teacher does not seek to extend such knowledge.	The teacher is fully aware of the resources available through the school or district to enhance own knowledge, to use in teaching, or for students who need them.	The teacher seeks out resources in and beyond the school or district in professional organizations, on the Internet, and in the community to enhance own knowledge, to use in teaching, and for students who need them.

Evidence

(continued)

Form G—*Continued*

Component	Unsatisfactory	Basic	Proficient	Distinguished
1e Designing Coherent Instruction	The series of learning experiences is poorly aligned with the instructional outcomes and does not represent a coherent structure. The experiences are suitable for only some students.	The series of learning experiences demonstrates partial alignment with instructional outcomes, some of which are likely to engage students in significant learning. The lesson or unit has a recognizable structure and reflects partial knowledge of students and resources.	The teacher coordinates knowledge of content, students, and resources to design a series of learning experiences aligned to instructional outcomes and suitable to groups of students. The lesson or unit has a clear structure and is likely to engage students in significant learning.	The teacher coordinates knowledge of content, students, and resources to design a series of learning experiences aligned to instructional outcomes, differentiated where appropriate to make them suitable for all students and likely to engage them in significant learning. The lesson or unit's structure is clear and allows for different pathways according to student needs.
Evidence				

Component	Unsatisfactory	Basic	Proficient	Distinguished
1f Designing Student Assessments	The teacher's plan for assessing student learning contains no clear criteria or standards, is poorly aligned with the instructional outcomes, or is inappropriate for many students. The results of assessment have minimal impact on the design of future instruction.	The teacher's plan for student assessment is partially aligned with the instructional outcomes, without clear criteria, and inappropriate for at least some students. The teacher intends to use assessment results to plan for future instruction for the class as a whole.	The teacher's plan for student assessment is aligned with the instructional outcomes, uses clear criteria, and is appropriate for the needs of students. The teacher intends to use assessment results to plan for future instruction for groups of students.	The teacher's plan for student assessment is fully aligned with the instructional outcomes, with clear criteria and standards that show evidence of student contribution to their development. Assessment methodologies may have been adapted for individuals, and the teacher intends to use assessment results to plan future instruction for individual students.
Evidence				

Domain 1: Planning and Preparation Rating: _____ U _____ B _____ P _____ D
(Rating is optional; if used, transfer rating to Form M: *Summary of Observations and Artifacts.*)

Domain 2: The Classroom Environment

Component	Unsatisfactory	Basic	Proficient	Distinguished
2a Creating an Environment of Respect and Rapport	Classroom interactions, both between the teacher and students and among students, are negative, inappropriate, or insensitive to students' cultural backgrounds, and characterized by sarcasm, put-downs, or conflict.	Classroom interactions, both between the teacher and students and among students, are generally appropriate and free from conflict, but may be characterized by occasional displays of insensitivity or lack of responsiveness to cultural or developmental differences among students.	Classroom interactions, both between teacher and students and among students, are polite and respectful, reflecting general warmth and caring, and are appropriate to the cultural and developmental differences among groups of students.	Classroom interactions among the teacher and individual students are highly respectful, reflecting genuine warmth and caring and sensitivity to students' cultures and levels of development. Students themselves ensure high levels of civility among members of the class.
Evidence				

Component	Unsatisfactory	Basic	Proficient	Distinguished
2b Establishing a Culture for Learning	The classroom environment conveys a negative culture for learning, characterized by low teacher commitment to the subject, low expectations for student achievement, and little or no student pride in work.	The teacher's attempts to create a culture for learning are partially successful, with little teacher commitment to the subject, modest expectations for student achievement, and little student pride in work. Both teacher and students appear to be only "going through the motions."	The classroom culture is characterized by high expectations for most students and genuine commitment to the subject by both teacher and students, with students demonstrating pride in their work.	High levels of student energy and teacher passion for the subject create a culture for learning in which everyone shares a belief in the importance of the subject and all students hold themselves to high standards of performance—for example, by initiating improvements to their work.
Evidence				

(*continued*)

Form G—*Continued*

Component	Unsatisfactory	Basic	Proficient	Distinguished
2c Managing Classroom Procedures	Much instructional time is lost because of inefficient classroom routines and procedures for transitions, handling of supplies, and performance of noninstructional duties.	Some instructional time is lost because classroom routines and procedures for transitions, handling of supplies, and performance of noninstructional duties are only partially effective.	Little instructional time is lost because of classroom routines and procedures for transitions, handling of supplies, and performance of noninstructional duties, which occur smoothly.	Students contribute to the seamless operation of classroom routines and procedures for transitions, handling of supplies, and performance of noninstructional duties.

Evidence

Component	Unsatisfactory	Basic	Proficient	Distinguished
2d Managing Student Behavior	There is no evidence that standards of conduct have been established, and little or no teacher monitoring of student behavior. Response to student misbehavior is repressive or disrespectful of student dignity.	It appears that the teacher has made an effort to establish standards of conduct for students. The teacher tries, with uneven results, to monitor student behavior and respond to student misbehavior.	Standards of conduct appear to be clear to students, and the teacher monitors student behavior against those standards. The teacher response to student misbehavior is appropriate and respects the students' dignity.	Standards of conduct are clear, with evidence of student participation in setting them. The teacher's monitoring of student behavior is subtle and preventive, and the teacher's response to student misbehavior is sensitive to individual student needs. Students take an active role in monitoring the standards of behavior.

Evidence

Component	Unsatisfactory	Basic	Proficient	Distinguished
2e Organizing Physical Space	The physical environment is unsafe, or some students don't have access to learning. There is poor alignment between the physical arrangement and the lesson activities.	The classroom is safe, and essential learning is accessible to most students; the teacher's use of physical resources, including computer technology, is moderately effective. The teacher may attempt to modify the physical arrangement to suit learning activities, with partial success.	The classroom is safe, and learning is accessible to all students; the teacher ensures that the physical arrangement is appropriate for the learning activities. The teacher makes effective use of physical resources, including computer technology.	The classroom is safe, and the physical environment ensures the learning of all students, including those with special needs. Students contribute to the use or adaptation of the physical environment to advance learning. Technology is used skillfully, as appropriate to the lesson.
Evidence				

(continued)

Domain 2: The Classroom Environment Rating ____ U ____ B ____ P ____ D

(Rating is optional; if used, transfer rating to Form M: *Summary of Observations and Artifacts*.)

Form G—*Continued*

Domain 3: Instruction

Component	Unsatisfactory	Basic	Proficient	Distinguished	
3a Communicating with Students	Expectations for learning, directions and procedures, and explanations of content are unclear or confusing to students. The teacher's use of language contains errors or is inappropriate for students' cultures or levels of development.	Expectations for learning, directions and procedures, and explanations of content are clarified after initial confusion; the teacher's use of language is correct but may not be completely appropriate for students' cultures or levels of development.	Expectations for learning, directions and procedures, and explanations of content are clear to students. Communications are appropriate for students' cultures and levels of development.	Expectations for learning, directions and procedures, and explanations of content are clear to students. The teacher's oral and written communication is clear and expressive, appropriate to students' cultures and levels of development, and anticipates possible student misconceptions.	

Evidence

Component	Unsatisfactory	Basic	Proficient	Distinguished	
3b Using Questioning and Discussion Techniques	The teacher's questions are low-level or inappropriate, eliciting limited student participation, and recitation rather than discussion.	Some of the teacher's questions elicit a thoughtful response, but most are low-level, posed in rapid succession. The teacher's attempts to engage all students in the discussion are only partially successful.	Most of the teacher's questions elicit a thoughtful response, and the teacher allows sufficient time for students to answer. All students participate in the discussion, with the teacher stepping aside when appropriate.	Questions reflect high expectations and are culturally and developmentally appropriate. Students formulate many of the high-level questions and ensure that all voices are heard.	

Evidence

Component	Unsatisfactory	Basic	Proficient	Distinguished
3c **Engaging Students in Learning**	Activities and assignments, materials, and groupings of students are inappropriate for the instructional outcomes or students' cultures or levels of understanding, resulting in little intellectual engagement. The lesson has no structure or is poorly paced.	Activities and assignments, materials, and groupings of students are partially appropriate for the instructional outcomes or students' cultures or levels of understanding, resulting in moderate intellectual engagement. The lesson has a recognizable structure but is not fully maintained.	Activities and assignments, materials, and groupings of students are fully appropriate for the instructional outcomes and students' cultures and levels of understanding. All students are engaged in work of a high level of rigor. The lesson's structure is coherent, with appropriate pace.	Students, throughout the lesson, are highly intellectually engaged in significant learning and make material contributions to the activities, student groupings, and materials. The lesson is adapted as needed to the needs of individuals, and the structure and pacing allow for student reflection and closure.
Evidence				

Component	Unsatisfactory	Basic	Proficient	Distinguished
3d **Using Assessment in Instruction**	Assessment is not used in instruction, either through monitoring of progress by the teacher or students, or feedback to students. Students are not aware of the assessment criteria used to evaluate their work.	Assessment is occasionally used in instruction, through some monitoring of progress of learning by the teacher and/or students. Feedback to students is uneven, and students are aware of only some of the assessment criteria used to evaluate their work.	Assessment is regularly used in instruction, through self-assessment by students, monitoring of progress of learning by the teacher and/or students, and high-quality feedback to students. Students are fully aware of the assessment criteria used to evaluate their work.	Assessment is used in a sophisticated manner in instruction, through student involvement in establishing the assessment criteria, self-assessment by students, monitoring of progress by both students and the teacher, and high-quality feedback to students from a variety of sources.
Evidence				

(continued)

Form G—*Continued*

Component	Unsatisfactory	Basic	Proficient	Distinguished
3e Demonstrating Flexibility and Responsiveness	The teacher adheres to the instruction plan, even when a change would improve the lesson or address students' lack of interest. The teacher brushes aside student questions; when students experience difficulty, the teacher blames the students or their home environment.	The teacher attempts to modify the lesson when needed and to respond to student questions, with moderate success. The teacher accepts responsibility for student success but has only a limited repertoire of strategies to draw upon.	The teacher promotes the successful learning of all students, making adjustments as needed to instruction plans and accommodating student questions, needs, and interests.	The teacher seizes an opportunity to enhance learning, building on a spontaneous event or student interests. The teacher ensures the success of all students, using an extensive repertoire of instructional strategies.
Evidence				

Domain 3: Instruction Rating _____ U _____ B _____ P _____ D

(Rating is optional; if used, transfer rating to Form M: *Summary of Observations and Artifacts*.)

Form G—*Continued*

Teacher _____ School _____

Strengths of the Lesson

Areas for Growth

We have participated in a conversation on the above items.

Teacher's signature _____Date _____

Administrator's signature _____Date _____

Form H
Evidence for Domain 4

Teacher _____ School _____ Date _____

Grade Level(s) _____ Subject(s) _____

Evaluator _____ School Year _____ – _____

Component	Evidence	Comments	Rating
4b: Maintaining Accurate Records	• • •		
4c: Communicating with Families	• • •		
4d: Participating in a Professional Community	• • •		
4e: Growing and Developing Professionally	• • •		
4f: Showing Professionalism	• • •		

Form H—*Continued*

Domain 4: Professional Responsibilities

Component	Unsatisfactory	Basic	Proficient	Distinguished
4b Maintaining Accurate Records	The teacher's systems for maintaining both instructional and noninstructional records are either nonexistent or in disarray, resulting in errors and confusion.	The teacher's systems for maintaining both instructional and noninstructional records are rudimentary and only partially effective.	The teacher's systems for maintaining both instructional and noninstructional records are accurate, efficient, and effective.	The teacher's systems for maintaining both instructional and noninstructional records are accurate, efficient, and effective, and students contribute to its maintenance.

Notes:

Component	Unsatisfactory	Basic	Proficient	Distinguished
4c Communicating with Families	The teacher's communication with families about the instructional program or about individual students is sporadic or culturally inappropriate. The teacher makes no attempt to engage families in the instructional program.	The teacher adheres to school procedures for communicating with families and makes modest attempts to engage families in the instructional program. But communications are not always appropriate to the cultures of those families.	The teacher communicates frequently with families and successfully engages them in the instructional program. Information to families about individual students is conveyed in a culturally appropriate manner.	The teacher's communication with families is frequent and sensitive to cultural traditions; students participate in the communication. The teacher successfully engages families in the instructional program, as appropriate.

Notes:

Component	Unsatisfactory	Basic	Proficient	Distinguished
4d Participating in a Professional Community	The teacher avoids participating in a professional community or in school and district events and projects; relationships with colleagues are negative or self-serving.	The teacher becomes involved in the professional community and in school and district events and projects when specifically asked; relationships with colleagues are cordial.	The teacher participates actively in the professional community and in school and district events and projects, and maintains positive and productive relationships with colleagues.	The teacher makes a substantial contribution to the professional community and to school and district events and projects, and assumes a leadership role among the faculty.

Notes:

(continued)

Form H—Continued

Component	Unsatisfactory	Basic	Proficient	Distinguished
4e **Growing and Developing Professionally**	The teacher does not participate in professional development activities and makes no effort to share knowledge with colleagues. The teacher is resistant to feedback from supervisors or colleagues.	The teacher participates in professional development activities that are convenient or are required, and makes limited contributions to the profession. The teacher accepts, with some reluctance, feedback from supervisors and colleagues.	The teacher seeks out opportunities for professional development based on an individual assessment of need and actively shares expertise with others. The teacher welcomes feedback from supervisors and colleagues.	The teacher actively pursues professional development opportunities and initiates activities to contribute to the profession. In addition, the teacher seeks feedback from supervisors and colleagues.

Notes:

Component	Unsatisfactory	Basic	Proficient	Distinguished
4f **Showing Professionalism**	The teacher has little sense of ethics and professionalism and contributes to practices that are self-serving or harmful to students. The teacher fails to comply with school and district regulations and time lines.	The teacher is honest and well intentioned in serving students and contributing to decisions in the school, but the teacher's attempts to serve students are limited. The teacher complies minimally with school and district regulations, doing just enough to get by.	The teacher displays a high level of ethics and professionalism in dealings with both students and colleagues and complies fully and voluntarily with school and district regulations.	The teacher is proactive and assumes a leadership role in making sure that school practices and procedures ensure that all students, particularly those traditionally underserved, are honored in the school. The teacher displays the highest standards of ethical conduct and takes a leadership role in seeing that colleagues comply with school and district regulations.

Notes:

Summary of Domain 4: Professional Responsibilities

Domain 4: Professional Responsibilities Rating: _____ U _____ B _____ P _____ D
(Rating is optional; if used, transfer rating to Form M: *Summary of Observations and Artifacts*.)

Form I

Self-Assessment of Practice

Teacher _____ School _____

Grade Level(s) _____ Subject(s) _____ Date _____

Directions: Consider your teaching practice and determine, for each component of the framework for teaching, the level of performance that best reflects your own assessment. Circle or highlight the appropriate words, and then transfer your judgments to the last page of this form. This will provide you with a summary of your current level of practice.

The final page may be combined with materials from other teachers in your school to determine the patterns of need across the school.

Domain I: Planning and Preparation

Component	Unsatisfactory	Basic	Proficient	Distinguished
Ia Demonstrating Knowledge of Content and Pedagogy	The teacher's plans and practice display little knowledge of the content, prerequisite relationships between different aspects of the content, or the instructional practices specific to that discipline.	The teacher's plans and practice reflect some awareness of the important concepts in the discipline, prerequisite relationships between them, and the instructional practices specific to that discipline.	The teacher's plans and practice reflect solid knowledge of the content, prerequisite relationships between important concepts, and the instructional practices specific to that discipline.	The teacher's plans and practice reflect extensive knowledge of the content and the structure of the discipline. The teacher actively builds on knowledge of prerequisites and misconceptions when describing instruction or seeking causes for student misunderstanding.
Ib Demonstrating Knowledge of Students	The teacher demonstrates little or no knowledge of students' backgrounds, cultures, skills, language proficiency, interests, and special needs, and does not seek such understanding.	The teacher indicates the importance of understanding students' backgrounds, cultures, skills, language proficiency, interests, and special needs, and attains this knowledge for the class as a whole.	The teacher actively seeks knowledge of students' backgrounds, cultures, skills, language proficiency, interests, and special needs, and attains this knowledge for groups of students.	The teacher actively seeks knowledge of students' backgrounds, cultures, skills, language proficiency, interests, and special needs from a variety of sources, and attains this knowledge for individual students.
Ic Setting Instructional Outcomes	Instructional outcomes are unsuitable for students, represent trivial or low-level learning, or are stated only as activities. They do not permit viable methods of assessment.	Instructional outcomes are of moderate rigor and are suitable for some students, but consist of a combination of activities and goals, some of which permit viable methods of assessment. They reflect more than one type of learning, but the teacher makes no attempt at coordination or integration.	Instructional outcomes are stated as goals reflecting high-level learning and curriculum standards. They are suitable for most students in the class, represent different types of learning, and can be assessed. The outcomes reflect opportunities for coordination.	Instructional outcomes are stated as goals that can be assessed, reflecting rigorous learning and curriculum standards. They represent different types of content, offer opportunities for both coordination and integration, and take account of the needs of individual students.

(continued)

Form I—*Continued*

Component	Unsatisfactory	Basic	Proficient	Distinguished
1d Demonstrating Knowledge of Resources	The teacher demonstrates little or no familiarity with resources to enhance own knowledge, to use in teaching, or for students who need them. The teacher does not seek such knowledge.	The teacher demonstrates some familiarity with resources available through the school or district to enhance own knowledge, to use in teaching, or for students who need them. The teacher does not seek to extend such knowledge.	The teacher is fully aware of the resources available through the school or district to enhance own knowledge, to use in teaching, or for students who need them.	The teacher seeks out resources in and beyond the school or district in professional organizations, on the Internet, and in the community to enhance own knowledge, to use in teaching, and for students who need them.
1e Designing Coherent Instruction	The series of learning experiences is poorly aligned with the instructional outcomes and does not represent a coherent structure. The experiences are suitable for only some students.	The series of learning experiences demonstrates partial alignment with instructional outcomes, and some of the experiences are likely to engage students in significant learning. The lesson or unit has a recognizable structure and reflects partial knowledge of students and resources.	The teacher coordinates knowledge of content, of students, and of resources to design a series of learning experiences aligned to instructional outcomes and suitable for groups of students. The lesson or unit has a clear structure and is likely to engage students in significant learning.	The teacher coordinates knowledge of content, of students, and of resources, to design a series of learning experiences aligned to instructional outcomes, differentiated where appropriate to make them suitable to all students and likely to engage them in significant learning. The lesson or unit structure is clear and allows for different pathways according to student needs.
1f Designing Student Assessments	The teacher's plan for assessing student learning contains no clear criteria or standards, is poorly aligned with the instructional outcomes, or is inappropriate for many students. The results of assessment have minimal impact on the design of future instruction.	The teacher's plan for student assessment is partially aligned with the instructional outcomes, without clear criteria, and inappropriate for at least some students. The teacher intends to use assessment results to plan for future instruction for the class as a whole.	The teacher's plan for student assessment is aligned with the instructional outcomes, uses clear criteria, and is appropriate to the needs of students. The teacher intends to use assessment results to plan for future instruction for groups of students.	The teacher's plan for student assessment is fully aligned with the instructional outcomes, with clear criteria and standards that show evidence of student contribution to their development. Assessment methodologies may have been adapted for individuals, and the teacher intends to use assessment results to plan future instruction for individual students.

Domain 2: The Classroom Environment

Component	Unsatisfactory	Basic	Proficient	Distinguished
2a Creating an Environment of Respect and Rapport	Classroom interactions, both between the teacher and students and among students, are negative, inappropriate, or insensitive to students' cultural backgrounds and are characterized by sarcasm, put-downs, or conflict.	Classroom interactions, both between the teacher and students and among students, are generally appropriate and free from conflict, but may be characterized by occasional displays of insensitivity or lack of responsiveness to cultural or developmental differences among students.	Classroom interactions between the teacher and students and among students are polite and respectful, reflecting general warmth and caring, and are appropriate to the cultural and developmental differences among groups of students.	Classroom interactions between the teacher and individual students are highly respectful, reflecting genuine warmth and caring and sensitivity to students' cultures and levels of development. Students themselves ensure high levels of civility among members of the class.
2b Establishing a Culture for Learning	The classroom environment conveys a negative culture for learning, characterized by low teacher commitment to the subject, low expectations for student achievement, and little or no student pride in work.	The teacher's attempt to create a culture for learning is partially successful, with little teacher commitment to the subject, modest expectations for student achievement, and little student pride in work. Both the teacher and students appear to be only "going through the motions."	The classroom culture is characterized by high expectations for most students and genuine commitment to the subject by both teacher and students, with students demonstrating pride in their work.	High levels of student energy and teacher passion for the subject create a culture for learning in which everyone shares a belief in the importance of the subject and all students hold themselves to high standards of performance—for example, by initiating improvements to their work.
2c Managing Classroom Procedures	Much instructional time is lost because of inefficient classroom routines and procedures for transitions, handling of supplies, and performance of noninstructional duties.	Some instructional time is lost because classroom routines and procedures for transitions, handling of supplies, and performance of noninstructional duties are only partially effective.	Little instructional time is lost because of classroom routines and procedures for transitions, handling of supplies, and performance of noninstructional duties, which occur smoothly.	Students contribute to the seamless operation of classroom routines and procedures for transitions, handling of supplies, and performance of noninstructional duties.

(continued)

Form I—*Continued*

Component	Unsatisfactory	Basic	Proficient	Distinguished
2d Managing Student Behavior	There is no evidence that standards of conduct have been established and little or no teacher monitoring of student behavior. Response to student misbehavior is repressive or disrespectful of student dignity.	It appears that the teacher has made an effort to establish standards of conduct for students. The teacher tries, with uneven results, to monitor student behavior and respond to student misbehavior.	Standards of conduct appear to be clear to students, and the teacher monitors student behavior against those standards. The teacher's response to student misbehavior is appropriate and respects the students' dignity.	Standards of conduct are clear, with evidence of student participation in setting them. The teacher's monitoring of student behavior is subtle and preventive, and the teacher's response to student misbehavior is sensitive to individual student needs. Students take an active role in monitoring the standards of behavior.
2e Organizing Physical Space	The physical environment is unsafe, or some students don't have access to learning. Alignment between the physical arrangement and the lesson activities is poor.	The classroom is safe, and essential learning is accessible to most students; the teacher's use of physical resources, including computer technology, is moderately effective. The teacher may attempt to modify the physical arrangement to suit learning activities, with partial success.	The classroom is safe, and learning is accessible to all students; the teacher ensures that the physical arrangement is appropriate to the learning activities. The teacher makes effective use of physical resources, including computer technology.	The classroom is safe, and the physical environment ensures the learning of all students, including those with special needs. Students contribute to the use or adaptation of the physical environment to advance learning. Technology is used skillfully, as appropriate to the lesson.

Domain 3: Instruction

Component	Unsatisfactory	Basic	Proficient	Distinguished
3a Communicating with Students	Expectations for learning, directions and procedures, and explanations of content are unclear or confusing to students. The teacher's use of language contains errors or is inappropriate for students' cultures or levels of development.	Expectations for learning, directions and procedures, and explanations of content are clarified after initial confusion; the teacher's use of language is correct but may not be completely appropriate for students' cultures or levels of development.	Expectations for learning, directions and procedures, and explanations of content are clear to students. Communications are appropriate for students' cultures and levels of development.	Expectations for learning, directions and procedures, and explanations of content are clear to students. The teacher's oral and written communication is clear and expressive, appropriate for students' cultures and levels of development, and anticipates possible student misconceptions.

Component	Unsatisfactory	Basic	Proficient	Distinguished
3b Using Questioning and Discussion Techniques	The teacher's questions are low-level or inappropriate, eliciting limited student participation and recitation rather than discussion.	Some of the teacher's questions elicit a thoughtful response, but most are low-level, posed in rapid succession. The teacher's attempts to engage all students in the discussion are only partially successful.	Most of the teacher's questions elicit a thoughtful response, and the teacher allows sufficient time for students to answer. All students participate in the discussion, with the teacher stepping aside when appropriate.	Questions reflect high expectations and are culturally and developmentally appropriate. Students formulate many of the high-level questions and ensure that all voices are heard.
3c Engaging Students in Learning	Activities and assignments, materials, and groupings of students are inappropriate for the instructional outcomes or students' cultures or levels of understanding, resulting in little intellectual engagement. The lesson has no structure or is poorly paced.	Activities and assignments, materials, and groupings of students are partially appropriate to the instructional outcomes or students' cultures or levels of understanding, resulting in moderate intellectual engagement. The lesson has a recognizable structure, but that structure is not fully maintained.	Activities and assignments, materials, and groupings of students are fully appropriate for the instructional outcomes and students' cultures and levels of understanding. All students are engaged in work of a high level of rigor. The lesson's structure is coherent, with appropriate pace.	Students, throughout the lesson, are highly intellectually engaged in significant learning, and make material contributions to the activities, student groupings, and materials. The lesson is adapted as necessary to the needs of individuals, and the structure and pacing allow for student reflection and closure.
3d Using Assessment in Instruction	Assessment is not used in instruction, either through monitoring of progress by the teacher or students, or through feedback to students. Students are unaware of the assessment criteria used to evaluate their work.	Assessment is occasionally used in instruction, through some monitoring of progress of learning by the teacher and/or students. Feedback to students is uneven, and students are aware of only some of the assessment criteria used to evaluate their work.	Assessment is regularly used in instruction, through self-assessment by students, monitoring of progress of learning by the teacher and/or students, and high-quality feedback to students. Students are fully aware of the assessment criteria used to evaluate their work.	Assessment is used in a sophisticated manner in instruction, through student involvement in establishing the assessment criteria, self-assessment by students, monitoring of progress by both students and teacher, and high-quality feedback to students from a variety of sources.
3e Demonstrating Flexibility and Responsiveness	The teacher adheres to the instruction plan, even when a change would improve the lesson or address students' lack of interest. The teacher brushes aside student questions; when students experience difficulty, the teacher blames the students or their home environment.	The teacher attempts to modify the lesson when needed and to respond to student questions, with moderate success. The teacher accepts responsibility for student success, but has only a limited repertoire of strategies to draw upon.	The teacher promotes the successful learning of all students, making adjustments as needed to instruction plans and accommodating student questions, needs, and interests.	The teacher seizes an opportunity to enhance learning, building on a spontaneous event or student interests. The teacher ensures the success of all students, using an extensive repertoire of instructional strategies.

(continued)

Form I—*Continued*

Domain 4: Professional Responsibilities

Component	Unsatisfactory	Basic	Proficient	Distinguished
4a Reflecting on Teaching	The teacher does not accurately assess the effectiveness of the lesson and has no ideas about how the lesson could be improved.	The teacher provides a partially accurate and objective description of the lesson but does not cite specific evidence. The teacher makes only general suggestions as to how the lesson might be improved.	The teacher provides an accurate and objective description of the lesson, citing specific evidence. The teacher makes some specific suggestions as to how the lesson might be improved.	The teacher's reflection on the lesson is thoughtful and accurate, citing specific evidence. The teacher draws on an extensive repertoire to suggest alternative strategies and predicts the likely success of each.
4b Maintaining Accurate Records	The teacher's systems for maintaining both instructional and noninstructional records are either nonexistent or in disarray, resulting in errors and confusion.	The teacher's systems for maintaining both instructional and noninstructional records are rudimentary and only partially effective.	The teacher's systems for maintaining both instructional and noninstructional records are accurate, efficient, and effective.	The teacher's systems for maintaining both instructional and noninstructional records are accurate, efficient, and effective, and students contribute to its maintenance.
4c Communicating with Families	The teacher's communication with families about the instructional program or about individual students is sporadic or culturally inappropriate. The teacher makes no attempt to engage families in the instructional program.	The teacher adheres to school procedures for communicating with families and makes modest attempts to engage families in the instructional program. But communications are not always appropriate to the cultures of those families.	The teacher communicates frequently with families and successfully engages them in the instructional program. Information to families about individual students is conveyed in a culturally appropriate manner.	The teacher's communication with families is frequent and sensitive to cultural traditions; students participate in the communication. The teacher successfully engages families in the instructional program, as appropriate.
4d Participating in a Professional Community	The teacher avoids participating in a professional community or in school and district events and projects; relationships with colleagues are negative or self-serving.	The teacher becomes involved in the professional community and in school and district events and projects when specifically asked; relationships with colleagues are cordial.	The teacher participates actively in the professional community and in school and district events and projects, and maintains positive and productive relationships with colleagues.	The teacher makes a substantial contribution to the professional community and to school and district events and projects, and assumes a leadership role among the faculty.

Component	Unsatisfactory	Basic	Proficient	Distinguished
4e Growing and Developing Professionally	The teacher does not participate in professional development activities and makes no effort to share knowledge with colleagues. The teacher is resistant to feedback from supervisors or colleagues.	The teacher participates in professional development activities that are convenient or are required, and makes limited contributions to the profession. The teacher accepts, with some reluctance, feedback from supervisors and colleagues.	The teacher seeks out opportunities for professional development based on an individual assessment of need and actively shares expertise with others. The teacher welcomes feedback from supervisors and colleagues.	The teacher actively pursues professional development opportunities and initiates activities to contribute to the profession. In addition, the teacher seeks feedback from supervisors and colleagues.
4f Showing Professionalism	The teacher has little sense of ethics and professionalism and contributes to practices that are self-serving or harmful to students. The teacher fails to comply with school and district regulations and time lines.	The teacher is honest and well intentioned in serving students and contributing to decisions in the school, but the teacher's attempts to serve students are limited. The teacher complies minimally with school and district regulations, doing just enough to get by.	The teacher displays a high level of ethics and professionalism in dealings with both students and colleagues and complies fully and voluntarily with school and district regulations.	The teacher is proactive and assumes a leadership role in making sure that school practices and procedures ensure that all students, particularly those traditionally underserved, are honored in the school. The teacher displays the highest standards of ethical conduct and takes a leadership role in seeing that colleagues comply with school and district regulations.

(continued)

Form I—*Continued*

Teacher _____   School _____

Grade Level(s) _____   Subject(s) _____   Date _____

U = Unsatisfactory   B = Basic   P = Proficient   D = Distinguished

	U	B	P	D
Domain 1: Planning and Preparation				
1a: Demonstrating Knowledge of Content and Pedagogy				
1b: Demonstrating Knowledge of Students				
1c: Setting Instructional Outcomes				
1d: Demonstrating Knowledge of Resources				
1e: Designing Coherent Instruction				
1f: Designing Student Assessments				
Domain 2: Classroom Environment	U	B	P	D
2a: Creating an Environment of Respect and Rapport				
2b: Establishing a Culture for Learning				
2c: Managing Classroom Procedures				
2d: Managing Student Behavior				
2e: Organizing Physical Space				

Domain 3: Instruction	U	B	P	D
3a: Communicating with Students				
3b: Using Questioning and Discussion Techniques				
3c: Engaging Students in Learning				
3d: Using Assessment in Instruction				
3e: Demonstrating Flexibility and Responsiveness				
Domain 4: Professional Responsibilities	U	B	P	D
4a: Reflecting on Teaching				
4b: Maintaining Accurate Records				
4c: Communicating with Families				
4d: Participating in a Professional Community				
4e: Growing and Developing Professionally				
4f: Showing Professionalism				

Form J
Individual Professional Development Plan

Teacher _____   School _____

Grade Level(s) _____   Subject(s) _____   Date _____

Based on your self-assessment, your administrator's input, and any school or district initiatives, what goal have you identified? What is an area of knowledge or skill that you would like to strengthen?	
Describe the connection between this goal and your teaching assignment.	
What would success on this goal look like? How will you know when you have achieved it? What would count as evidence of success?	

Describe the activities you will do to work toward your goal, and their time lines.

Activity	Time Line

What resources will you need to better achieve your goal?

Form K

Individual Professional Development Log of Activities

Note: Complete one log for each goal identified in your individual professional development plan.

Teacher _____ School _____

Grade Level(s) _____ Subject(s) _____ Date _____

Goal _____

Date	Activity	Benefit

Form L
Reflection on the Individual Professional Development Plan

Name _____ Date _____

Goal _____

Write a separate reflection for each goal you have pursued this year. Each reflection should be no more than five paragraphs. It is intended to provide insights into your work during the year.

1. To what extent did you achieve your goal?

2. Did you find it necessary to modify your goal or your IPDP as you learned more?

3. Which of the activities on your IPDP did you find most useful? Did you do some activities that you had not initially planned? If so, what were they?

4. In what ways were your colleagues helpful to you in working toward your goal?

5. For Years 1 and 2 of the evaluation cycle only: Do you intend to continue working on this goal next year? Why or why not?

Form M
Summary of Observations and Artifacts

Teacher _____ School _____

Grade Level(s) _____ Subject(s) _____

Domain	Observation Dates				Artifacts
	1 __/__/____	2 __/__/____	3 __/__/____	Informal __/__/____	
1: Planning and Preparation					
2: The Classroom Environment					
3: Instruction					
4: Professional Responsibilities					

Summary of Performance

Domain 1

Domain 2

Domain 3

Domain 4

Form N
Annual Evaluation 1

Teacher _____ School _____

Grade Level(s) _____ Subject(s) _____

Evaluator _____ Date _____

Teacher's Status: _____ Probationary Year 1 _____ Year 2 _____ Year 3 _____ Year 4 _____
                  _____ Continuing _____ Regular Substitute _____ Part Time

Areas of Strength

Areas for Further Development

_____   _____   _____
              Teacher   Meets or Exceeds   Does Not Meet

expectations for teaching in the _____ School District.

_____   _____
        Teacher's Signature*   Evaluator's Signature

*Teacher's signature indicates only that the teacher has read this report.

Form O
Annual Evaluation 2

Teacher _____ School _____

Grade Level(s) _____ Subject(s) _____

Evaluator _____ Date _____

Teacher's Status _____ Probationary Year   1   2   3   _____ Tenured   Year of Employment _____
                                                  Circle

Domain 1: Planning and Preparation
Domain 2: The Classroom Environment
Domain 3: Instruction
Domain 4: Professional Responsibilities

Areas for Further Development

_____   _____   _____
                         Teacher   Meets or Exceeds   Does Not Meet

expectations for teaching in the _____ School District.

_____   _____
           Teacher's Signature*   Evaluator's Signature

*Teacher's signature indicates only that the teacher has read this report.

Appendix B:
Artifacts of Teaching

The observation of classroom performance is the most direct method whereby an observer (whether a mentor, an instructional coach, or a supervisor) can obtain evidence of a teacher's classroom skills. But as important as classroom practice is, it does not reflect the entirety of a teacher's responsibilities; some of those don't occur in the classroom at all. For example, an observer will never, even with multiple classroom observations, know how skilled a teacher is in communicating with families or participating in a professional community.

These other aspects of classroom teaching require artifacts. As part of a comprehensive program of mentoring or teacher evaluation, evidence of those nonclassroom tasks is needed so that a mentor or a supervisor can support the teacher in the full range of teaching responsibilities.

A collection of artifacts is sometimes called a "portfolio." Although the term is accurate, it is not used here, simply because in some settings it is also used to refer to teachers' collections of items that provide a total picture of their teaching, including videos, photographs of their classroom, their statement of educational philosophy, and other components. Teachers frequently develop these portfolios as part of their professional preparation and may use them as a visual résumé when applying for a teaching position. In such portfolios, appearance is important, because the teacher candidate is striving to make a positive impression on potential reviewers of the portfolio.

In contrast, the artifacts collected to demonstrate skill in the various components of the framework for teaching may not be finished products. Teachers assemble them in order to frame a conversation regarding some aspect of practice. Artifacts are intended to stimulate discussion, reflection, and professional learning. Although they should not be slap-dash, the artifacts should not be regarded as show pieces.

If artifacts are used in a teacher evaluation system, it is essential to spell out the expectations for both the number of items and their scope. It is not sufficient, for example, to ask teachers to provide evidence of how they communicate with families, even if the evaluation documents suggest some of the items that could be collected. A teacher might assemble 3 or 4 items only to discover that a colleague has collected 14! Such a situation causes anxiety and does not support professional conversation. Therefore, it is important that teachers know what is expected, so they can concentrate on the quality of what they collect.

The artifacts described here, and the components of the framework for teaching for which they provide evidence, are the following.

Unit Plan, with Student Assessment

This artifact provides evidence of a teacher's skill in long-range planning.
Components: 1a, 1b, 1c, 1d, 1e, and 1f

Activity or Assignment

This artifact is an assignment or directions for an activity, including student work, with the teacher's comments to students on their work. It provides excellent evidence of a teacher's skill in designing work that engages students in rigorous intellectual activity.
Components: 1a, 1b, 1c, 1e, 1f, 3c, 3d

Communication with Families

This artifact provides evidence of the range of techniques used by a teacher in communicating with families.
Components: 1b, 4c

Instructional and Noninstructional Records

This artifact provides evidence of a teacher's skill in maintaining accurate records, for both instructional and noninstructional matters.
Component: 4b

Participation in a Professional Community

This artifact provides evidence of a teacher's involvement in and commitment to the school as a professional organization.
Component: 4d

Professional Development

This artifact provides evidence of the teacher's participation in opportunities for professional learning and for sharing expertise with colleagues.
Component: 4e

Evidence of Student Learning

This artifact provides evidence of the teacher's effectiveness with students.

Components: All

At the end of each set of artifact documents is a feedback guide that an evaluator (or mentor, coach, or supervisor) can fill out and use in discussions with the teacher.

Unit Plan, with Student Assessment

Provide a plan for a unit of study that you will be using this school year, including its assessment. Attach any worksheets, assignments, or other materials that students will be using in the unit.

For the unit as a whole, complete the Planning Guide (Figure B.1), specifying the major concepts being addressed in the unit, the overall assessments used, and a summary of the types of activities that you will use to engage students in the content. On the Planning Grid (Figure B.2), briefly indicate (for each day of the unit) the topic to be addressed, a summary of the activities to be used, how students will be grouped, and the materials used.

Links to the Framework for Teaching

A unit plan is related to the following components in the framework for teaching:

1a: Demonstrating Knowledge of Content and Pedagogy
1b: Demonstrating Knowledge of Students
1c: Setting Instructional Outcomes
1d: Demonstrating Knowledge of Resources
1e: Designing Coherent Instruction
1f: Designing Student Assessments

Guidance

As you prepare the unit and consider the questions for discussion, you will find that a good unit is one that demonstrates the following:

• Your knowledge of content, including knowledge of prerequisite relationships, links to other disciplines, and state and district content standards
• Clear criteria and procedures for assessing student learning that enable students to monitor their own learning and that allow the teacher to plan for future instruction
• Your knowledge of students' backgrounds, skills, and interests
• Clear goals for student learning
• A variety of learning activities that promote student engagement in learning and that develop important concepts from simpler to more complex

See Figure B.3 for a feedback guide to use in discussing the unit plan.

Figure B.1

Planning Guide

For the unit as a whole, respond to the following questions.

1. What are your goals for your students? What do you intend for them to learn? What are the essential questions that your students will be able to understand and answer as a result of this unit?

2. How do you know that this unit is appropriate for the students in your class?

3. How will students demonstrate their learning? What will they do as a result of engaging with this unit? Attach your plan for assessing student learning.

4. How does the unit support the state or district's content standards?

5. What are the connections between this unit and other disciplines?

6. What prerequisite knowledge or skill must students have in order to be successful in this unit? What is your evidence that your students have this understanding?

7. How does your plan for this unit help students develop understanding of the unit's important concepts? How does it help correct or avoid common student misconceptions about this topic?

8. What adjustments do you make, or have you made in the past, for individual students in the class?

Figure B.2
Planning Grid

Teacher _____ School _____

Grade Level _____ Subject _____ Unit Topic _____

Directions: For each day of the unit, indicate the topic you plan to address, a summary of the activities you intend to use, how students will be grouped, and the materials you plan to use.

	Monday	Tuesday	Wednesday	Thursday	Friday
Week 1					
Week 2					
Week 3					

Figure B.3

Feedback Guide for the Unit Plan

Characteristic	Little or None	Moderate	Extensive
The teacher's unit of study demonstrates the following (as appropriate): Knowledge of content, including . . . • Important concepts to be learned • The structure of the discipline • Prerequisite relationships among the various concepts • Links to other disciplines • Relationship with the state's or district's content standards • Frequent student misconceptions			
Knowledge of students, including their . . . • Knowledge and skill • Interests and cultural backgrounds • Approaches to learning			
Learning goals that reflect . . . • Learning needs of students in the class • Important learning in the discipline • Goals rather than activities • A range of *types* of objectives (e.g., knowledge, reasoning, group skill, communication)			
Learning activities that. . . • Are intended to achieve the learning goals • Are likely to engage students in thinking and reasoning • Represent a variety of approaches			
Criteria and procedures for assessing student learning that are . . . • Suitable to the learning goals • Appropriate to students' levels of development			
The unit as a whole . . . • Has a coherent structure, with the development of more complex ideas building on simpler ones • Incorporates the use of technology, as appropriate • Is suitable for diverse learners			

Activity or Assignment

Provide activity directions or an assignment that engages students in learning an important concept. This might be a homework assignment, a worksheet, project guidelines, or a problem to solve. After looking at student papers, select several examples of student work in response to the assignment. These examples should reflect the full range of student ability in the class and should include any feedback you offered to students on their work.

Be prepared to discuss the following questions, as appropriate:

1. What is the concept you intend for your students to learn or explore?

2. How does this assignment fit within the prior and future learning of students in this class?

3. Why did you decide to organize the assignment in this manner? That is, how does this approach advance student understanding?

4. Consider the student work, both that of the class as a whole and that of those students for whom you have samples:

   • What does it tell you about their level of understanding?
   • What does it say about their perseverance?

5. If you had the opportunity to make this same assignment again, would you do it in the same way? If not, how might you alter it, and why?

6. Given the student work, what do you plan to do next with these students?

Links to the Framework for Teaching

An instructional artifact, and the accompanying student work and teacher commentary, is related to the following components in the framework for teaching:

1a:Demonstrating Knowledge of Content and Pedagogy
1b:Demonstrating Knowledge of Students
1c:Setting Instructional Outcomes
1e:Designing Coherent Instruction
1f:Designing Student Assessments
3c:Engaging Students in Learning
3d:Using Assessment in Instruction

Guidance

As you collect your samples and consider the questions, you will find that a good assignment is one that demonstrates the following:

- Your knowledge of content and the important concepts for students to learn
- Your knowledge of students' skills and knowledge
- Clarity of goals for student learning
- Design of a learning activity that promotes student engagement in learning
- Feedback to individual students to help them develop deeper understanding
- Use of student work as a formative assessment to plan future learning

See Figure B.4 for a feedback guide to use when discussing an activity or assignment.

Figure B.4

Feedback Guide for the Activity or Assignment

Characteristic	Little or None	Moderate	Extensive
The teacher's activity or assignment and student work (with teacher feedback) demonstrate the following (as appropriate): Quality of the assignment, including . . . • Importance of the concepts being learned • Alignment with instructional goals • Cognitive challenge asked of students • Clarity of directions • Suitability for diverse learners			
Engagement of students in the task, including . . . • Quality of student thinking • Successful completion of the task • Evidence of learning from the assignment			
Teacher feedback to students reflects . . . • Knowledge of learning needs of students in the class • High quality, with specificity and focus on learning			
Reflection on the activity indicates . . . • Accurate assessment of the success of the activity • Planning for further learning for students			

Communication with Families

Collect three samples of communication with families of the students you teach. These should represent the full range of *types* of communication you have with families and should include communication about both instructional and noninstructional topics. If appropriate, the communication should be two-way.

Examples of artifacts you might collect include the following:

- Course syllabus
- Class newsletter
- Handouts for back-to-school night
- Grading policies you send home to families
- Information regarding a new program
- Activities for parents to do with their children at home
- Completed family contact log
- A note to a parent (with all identifying information removed)
- A note from a parent (with all identifying information removed)
- Directions for families about a class trip
- Guidelines for a project (for example, the science fair) if families are expected to be involved
- Student assignments incorporating information from the home or community (such as interviewing older neighbors or relatives, graphing numbers of different types of furniture in the home)
- Information about an upcoming school or class concert or other event
- Information for families about "math night" or a guest speaker
- Schedule for individual parent conferences
- Guidelines for students and parents regarding student-led conferences
- Information for parents on how to look at a student's portfolio with their children

Be prepared to discuss the following questions, as appropriate:

1. What role does communicating with families play in your instructional program?

2. How do you encourage two-way communication with the families of your students?

3. To what extent do you adapt your message to the cultural or social backgrounds of the students in your class?

4. To what extent do you encounter a language barrier in communicating with families? If so, how do you address it?

5. What other challenges do you confront in communication with families? How have you addressed those challenges?

Links to the Framework for Teaching

Examples of communication with families are related to the following components in the framework for teaching:

    1b: Demonstrating Knowledge of Students

    4c: Communicating with Families

Guidance

As you collect your samples and consider the questions, you will find that your best communications are ones that demonstrate the following:

- Clarity of language
- Knowledge of students' skills and knowledge, interests, and backgrounds
- Sensitivity to the cultures and backgrounds of students and their families
- Information about the instructional program communicated in a manner that is comprehensible to noneducators
- Skill in engaging families in their children's learning
- Honesty about students' progress or behavior, combined with respect for parent concerns

See Figure B.5 for a feedback guide to use when discussing communication with families.

Figure B.5

Feedback Guide for Communicating with Families

Characteristic	Little or None	Moderate	Extensive
The teacher's communication with families about the program and individual students demonstrates the following (as appropriate): • Information about the instructional program • Variety of information about the instructional program • Range of *types* of communication • Appropriate frequency			
Knowledge of students, including . . . • Learning characteristics and challenges • Different approaches to learning • Level of performance in learning			
Appropriate use of language, including . . . • Clarity of language • Sensitivity to families' cultural backgrounds • Use of nontechnical language or jargon			
Respect for students' families, through . . . • Active listening during a conference • Prompt replies to parent requests or concerns • Respectful tone in both oral and written communication			
Participation of students . . . • In the preparation of materials for families • During a student-led conference			

Instructional and Noninstructional Records

Maintaining accurate records is an important aspect of good teaching. Instructional records are essential for teachers to know which students have attained a high level of understanding or skill and which students may need additional attention. Noninstructional records permit teachers to know, for example, when all students' permission slips for a field trip have been returned, or which students have volunteered to tutor younger students.

Assemble two samples of how you maintain accurate records, one instructional and one noninstructional. These may take any form that you find useful, and they may be simple, but they should be effective.

   Be prepared to discuss the following questions, as appropriate:

   1. How did you determine the approach or approaches you use?
   2. What makes the approach or approaches you use effective?
   3. What role, if any, did students play in developing the system?
   4. What role, if any, do students play in using the system?
   5. In what way would you like to improve your system for record keeping?

Links to the Framework for Teaching

   Your instructional and noninstructional records are directly related to the following component in the framework for teaching:
   4b: Maintaining Accurate Records

Guidance

   As you collect your records and consider the questions, you will find that your best records are those that demonstrate that following:

   • Clear procedures for ensuring accuracy
   • Opportunities for students to assist in maintaining the system
   • Anticipation of the likely uses for the information in the future, such as assigning grades or following up with parents

   See Figure B.6 for a feedback guide to use in discussing instructional and noninstructional records.

Figure B.6

Feedback Guide for Instructional and Noninstructional Records

Characteristic	Little or None	Moderate	Extensive
A teacher's instructional and noninstructional records demonstrate the following characteristics (as appropriate): Systems that . . . • Are accurate • Result in timely recording of information			
Evidence of student involvement in . . . • Developing the record-keeping systems • Maintaining the record-keeping systems			

Participation in a Professional Community

How have you actively participated in your professional community over the past year? Examples might be participating in a lesson study with colleagues, serving on a curriculum committee or a site council, participating in a district initiative, organizing a club for students, or making a presentation to parents on a school project. You may choose to keep track of them on the Professional Community Log (Figure B.7).

Be prepared to discuss the following questions, as appropriate:

1. How did you determine which areas to become involved in?
2. What important work of the school or the district were you able to advance through your participation?
3. What did you learn about the profession of teaching, or about your own practice, from this involvement?
4. What would you plan to do next year in this area?

Links to the Framework for Teaching

Your record of contributions to the school and the district is directly related to the following component in the framework for teaching:

4d: Participating in a Professional Community

Depending on what the involvement was, it might also have reflected other components. For example, preparing for a parent presentation would require that a teacher acquire and demonstrate knowledge of students' interests and cultural heritage.

Guidance

As you document evidence of your involvement in the school's professional community, you will find that the strongest collection is one that demonstrates the following:

• Willingness to participate in school events
• Leadership with colleagues

See Figure B.8 for a feedback guide to use in discussing participation in a professional community.

Figure B.7
Professional Community Log

Name _____ School _____ School Year _____–_____

Date	**Activity** (e.g., professional collaboration, series of committee meetings, presentation)	**Contribution**

Figure B.8

Feedback Guide for Participating in a Professional Community

Characteristic	Little or None	Moderate	Extensive
The teacher's participation in a professional community demonstrates the following characteristics (as appropriate): Participation in school affairs that . . . • Is active and freely given • Reflects a leadership role with colleagues • Is supportive of the school's mission for student learning			
Relationships with colleagues that . . . • Are mutually supportive and respectful • Demonstrate leadership in instructional affairs			
Contribution to the school's community of inquiry that . . . • Reflects the needs of the school • Is built on the assumption of every teacher's obligation toward ongoing learning			

Professional Development

What professional development activities have you participated in? The activities you take part in should be based on identified needs (perhaps as discovered using Form I: Self-Assessment of Practice in Appendix A) or on some other systematic approach.

Make some notes on the Professional Development Needs Analysis (Figure B.9). As you undertake professional development activities, keep track of what you have done and what you have learned on the Professional Development Log (Figure B.10).

Be prepared to discuss the following questions, as appropriate:

1. How did you determine which areas to focus on?
2. Which professional development activities did you find most valuable?
3. How were you able to incorporate what you learned into practice?

Links to the Framework for Teaching

Your record of professional development activities is related to the following component in the framework for teaching:

4e: Growing and Developing Professionally

Guidance

As you assemble your evidence of professional development, you will find that the strongest collection will include items that demonstrate the following:

- Enhancement of skills based on identified needs
- Service to the profession
- Clear analysis of how the learning can be applied to your own teaching

See Figure B.11 for a feedback guide to use in discussing professional development.

Figure B.9

Professional Development Needs Analysis

As you consider your priorities for professional development, consider the following questions.

1. Based on your self-assessment (using Form 1 in Appendix A or its equivalent), which areas of the framework for teaching would you most like to strengthen?

2. What other general instructional strategies (such as differentiation, cooperative learning, writing across the curriculum) have you become aware of and would you like to know more about?

3. What resources are available to you to learn more about an area of interest to you? Which of your colleagues are particularly knowledgeable? What books or articles are accessible?

Figure B.10
Professional Development Log

Name _____ School _____ School Year _____–_____

Date	Event (e.g., workshop, conference, class)	Benefits

Figure B.11

Feedback Guide for Professional Development

Characteristic	Little or None	Moderate	Extensive
A teacher's participation in professional development activities demonstrates the following characteristics (as appropriate): Selection of areas for work that is . . . • Based on identified needs • Linked to available resources • Aligned to needs of school/district			
Professional development activities (as reported in log) that . . . • Support identified needs • Represent a range of types of activities • Make use of the expertise of colleagues			
Benefits derived from professional development activities that . . . • Represent thoughtful reflection • Are linked to enhancement of skill in teaching students • Suggest further development activities			

Evidence of Student Learning

Because student learning is the goal of every teacher, it is important for teachers to be able to document the learning of the students under their charge. The activity presented here enables teachers to demonstrate their impact on their students. It is designed so that teachers, in consultation with their supervisors or coaches, determine the learning goals for which they want to collect evidence, and the nature of that evidence.

1. Determine which learning outcome you will focus on in your collection of evidence of student learning. The outcome should be important but not vague—for example, use of powerful language in persuasive writing or data analysis in social studies or science.

2. Determine how student proficiency on the outcome might be assessed. Locate or develop a performance task and a rubric by which to assess your students. If available, this assessment of student learning could be your district-developed end-of-course assessment. But it would have to be appropriate for the outcome you have selected and would have to be available at both the beginning and the end of the school year. In the case of assessing language use in persuasive writing, this task could simply be an assignment that requires students to write a letter to the editor of a magazine in September and another in May.

Note: It is preferable to administer the assessments during the course of instruction, to minimize the impact on daily class routine. In addition, the assessment can yield important formative information for a teacher.

3. Select students to be included in your sample. These are the students for whom you will collect and analyze pre- and post-instruction assessment data. This sample need not be an entire class, but it should include at least two students in each of three groups. The groups may reflect any number of dimensions—for example, students of high (or low) general ability or students who are language learners. Identify these students on the form titled Groups for Analysis (Figure B.12).

4. Administer the pre-instruction assessment, doing so in the course of normal instruction, if possible. For the students identified on Figure B.12, calculate the average score of the students in each of the three groups, using the rubric or scoring guide; enter these on the form titled Assessment Results (Figure B.13).

5. Teach throughout the year, focusing as appropriate, on the outcomes selected for analysis.

6. Toward the end of the year, administer the post-instruction assessment, doing so in the course of normal instruction, if possible. For the students identified on the Groups for Analysis form, calculate the average scores of students in the three groups; using the same rubric or scoring guide as for the pre-instruction assessment; enter these on the Assessment Results form (Figure B.13).

7. Calculate the gains (or losses) of students in the three groups. Enter these on the Assessment Results form.

8. Reflect on your learning as a result of this activity; record your thoughts on the form titled Reflection on Assessment Results (Figure B.14, p. 171). Be prepared to discuss your answers, as appropriate.

Links to the Framework for Teaching

Evidence of student learning relates to a number of components in the framework for teaching:

1b: Demonstrating Knowledge of Students

1c: Setting Instructional Outcomes

1f: Designing Student Assessments

3c: Engaging Students in Learning

3d: Using Assessment in Instruction

4a: Reflecting on Teaching

Guidance

As you collect and analyze data on student learning and consider the questions, you will find that your best analysis is that which demonstrates the following:

- Setting of important instructional goals
- Determination of appropriate evidence of student learning
- Establishment of important criteria on which to base the formation of groups of students for analysis
  - Accurate analysis of student achievement data
  - Thoughtful reflection on the implications of the analysis

See Figure B.15 for a feedback guide to use in discussing evidence of student learning.

Figure B.12

Groups for Analysis

Teacher _____ School _____

Grade/Class _____ Subject _____ School Year _____–_____

Student Learning Outcome _____

Names of Students	General Reasons for Grouping Students (e.g., by skill or ability level, language proficiency)
Group 1	
Group 2	
Group 3	

Figure B.13
Assessment Results

Teacher _____ School _____

Grade/Class _____ Subject _____ School Year _____–_____

Group 1 *Group Average:*		
Pre-instruction Assessment	**Post-instruction Assessment**	**Gain (or Loss)**

Group 2 *Group Average:*		
Pre-instruction Assessment	**Post-instruction Assessment**	**Gain (or Loss)**

Group 3 *Group Average:*		
Pre-instruction Assessment	**Post-instruction Assessment**	**Gain (or Loss)**

Comments: _____

Figure B.14
Reflection on Assessment Results

Teacher _____ School _____

Grade/Class _____ Subject _____ School Year _____–_____

Student Learning Outcome _____

1. What patterns did you observe in student learning? For example, did all students make similar gains in their learning, or were you more successful with some groups of students than with others?

2. What changes, if any, do you plan to make in future lessons so that all groups of students receive maximum benefit?

Figure B.15

Feedback Guide for Evidence of Student Learning

Characteristic	Little or None	Moderate	Extensive
A teacher's collection and analysis of data regarding student learning demonstrates the following (as appropriate): Quality of learning outcomes, as indicated by their . . . • Being stated clearly, as learning outcomes, not activities • Representing important, rather than trivial, learning			
Evidence of student learning that is aligned with the outcomes			
Quality of analysis of student learning gains, as indicated by . . . • Including sensible rationale for assignment of students to groups • Being convincing and substantiated by the evidence			
Quality of reflection on the experience, as indicated by . . . • Accuracy of the reflection • Likelihood that reflection will lead to thoughtful modifications of practice			

Index

Note: The letter *f* following a page number denotes a figure. A page number in **boldface** indicates location of a form.

About the Author

 Charlotte Danielson is an educational consultant based in Princeton, New Jersey. She has taught at all levels, from kindergarten through college, and has worked as an administrator, a curriculum director, and a staff developer in school districts in several regions of the United States. In addition, Danielson has served as a consultant to hundreds of school districts, universities, intermediate agencies, and state departments of education in virtually every state and in many other countries. In her consulting work, Danielson has specialized in aspects of teacher quality and evaluation, curriculum planning, performance assessment, and professional development. Her work has ranged from the training of practitioners to aspects of instruction and assessment, to the design of instruments and procedures for teacher evaluation, to keynote presentations at major conferences. For several years she served on the staff of the Educational Testing Service and was involved with many significant projects, including designing the assessor training program for Praxis III: Classroom Performance Assessments.

Danielson is the author of several books for teachers and administrators. These include *Enhancing Professional Practice: A Framework for Teaching* (1996, 2007), the Professional Inquiry Kit *Teaching for Understanding* (1996), *Teacher Evaluation to Enhance Professional Practice* (in collaboration with Tom McGreal, 2000), *Enhancing Student Achievement: A Framework for School Improvement* (2002), and *Teacher Leadership That Strengthens Professional Practice* (2006), all published by ASCD. In addition, she has written several *Collections of Performance Tasks and Rubrics*, published by Eye on Education. Charlotte Danielson may be reached at charlotte_danielson@hotmail.com.

Preparing Booklets from Multiple-Page Forms

Use your school's photocopier to make booklets from the multiple-page forms in this book. After making the prototype booklets, it will be easy to make duplicates.

At the copier, select 11" x 17" (ledger) paper and choose 2-sided copies. Orient the top of the pages to the top of the photocopier's glass.

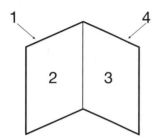

For a 4-page booklet, photocopy the pages in this order:

1, 4 and then 2, 3 on the reverse.

Fold the pages (in the center) vertically for a small booklet.

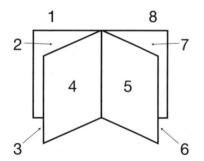

For an 8-page booklet, photocopy the pages in this order:

1, 8 and then 2, 7 on the reverse. Remove the photocopied pages.

3, 6 and then 4, 5 on reverse. Remove photocopied pages.

Place page 3 over page 1, fold all pages in the center (vertically) and staple, if desired.

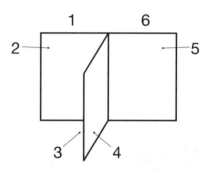

For a 6-page booklet, use 11" x 17" (ledger) paper to photocopy these pages in this order:

1, 6 and then 2, 5 on reverse. Fold the paper in half vertically.

For the interior pages, photocopy pages 3 and 4 (back-to-back) on an 8 1/2" x 11" sheet. Insert this page between pages 2 and 5—page 3 should face page 2.

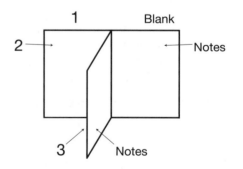

For a booklet with an odd number of pages to be photocopied, you may choose to insert a title page for page 1, insert a Notes page where appropriate, or leave the back (last) page blank.